GLASGOW
MEMORIES

The publishers would like to thank the following companies for their

support in the production of this book

Cardowan Creameries Ltd

The Denholm Group

J&M Murdoch & Son Ltd

Ross and Liddell

Southern Coaches

Whyte & Mackay

First published in Great Britain by True North Books Limited
England HX3 6SN
01422 244555
www.truenorthbooks.com
Copyright © True North Books Limited, 2014

GLASGOW
MEMORIES

CONTENTS

INTRODUCTION

For all of us, memories are the currency which we use to record the changes and progress in our everyday lives and to fix our place as individuals in the greater scheme of things. This is the latest publication in our 'Memories' series of publications, covering nostalgic reflections of towns and cities throughout the UK. In this new book we will be meandering through a pictorial cross-section of life in Glasgow over the last 100 years or so, to help satisfy the longing we all get from time to time, to recall memories of a different era that now seems better or simpler.

As we get older it is often easier to take a step back, and to view events and developments with a clearer sense of prospective. Our aim has been to assist in this respect by presenting a publication relevant to the area capable of rekindling memories of days gone by in an entertaining and informative manner. Looking through the pages of this book it is interesting to reflect on exactly how much change has taken place in the area over a short period, relative to its long history. Many of these photographs are unique and will inevitably remind us of experiences and events in our lives, of our families and of those whose influence and support has touched us to a greater or lesser degree.

Defining features about nostalgia are universal and can bring back fond memories from a time gone by. Recent research shows that nostalgia can counteract loneliness, boredom and anxiety. Couples feel closer and look happier when they're sharing nostalgic memories. People generally get a 'Warm Glow' inside when relating to events and occasions in the past and enjoy reminiscences about how things used to be – even when these events sometimes have a painful side. When people speak wistfully of the past, they typically become more optimistic and inspired about the future.

We can all remember events surrounding friends and family, holidays, weddings, special occasions and nights out in Glasgow. So let your mind wander and think of the youthful days at the dance hall or courting in one of the many cinemas in the city. Be entertained as we take you on a sentimental journey through the pages of 'Glasgow' Memories…. Happy Memories!

TEXT	TONY LAX, ANDREW MITCHELL, STEVE AINSWORTH
PHOTOGRAPH RESEARCH	TONY LAX
DESIGNER	SEAMUS MOLLOY
BUSINESS DEVELOPMENT MANAGER	PETER HOWARD

EVENTS & OCCASIONS

On the right is a picture you don't see every day! Sixteen Chipperfields Circus elephants in convoy through the packed crowds at Gorbals Cross, in 1952. It was the memory of a lifetime for us weans. After the parade everyone went to "Glesga Green" and watched them after setting up with all the free displays of animals. The name 'Chipperfield' dates back to James Chipperfield, who introduced performing animals to England at the Frost Fair on the Thames in 1684. After World War II, it became one of the biggest circuses in Europe, with a tent that could hold 6,000 people. The elephants were always a big attraction and not something you saw everyday in Glasgow. In those days before every house had a television, a visiting circus was a big deal. The other big names were Billy Smart and Bertram Mills. But could the 'human cannon ball' compete today with an X Box football game or a Mario Cart Space Race?...somehow we doubt it. Today, attitudes have changed and it is more about the acrobatics of the performers at shows like the Moscow State Circus.

With the appearance of a Hornby Doublo engine, the locomotive below was dwarfed by the mighty crane that lifted it into the air above the dockside of the River Clyde. The first heavy lift crane to be installed in Glasgow Harbour was the Clyde Villa crane at the western end of Plantation Quay, capable of lifting up to 60 tons. A crane is shown here loading railway locomotives built by the North British Locomotive Company onto a freighter for export.

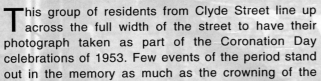

This group of residents from Clyde Street line up across the full width of the street to have their photograph taken as part of the Coronation Day celebrations of 1953. Few events of the period stand out in the memory as much as the crowning of the young Queen Elizabeth II. Later they would be attending one of hundreds of street parties taking place throughout the city. Trestle tables and benches were borrowed and mums slaved away all day making lots of goodies, including fairy cakes, potted meat

sandwiches, jelly and ice cream. Joyful scenes, rivalling those witnessed on VE Day took place in every village. The girls dressed in white dresses with red white and blue sashes and the boys dressed in their Sunday best, on what was a special day. Those lucky enough to have a television set suddenly found themselves to be very popular. Neighbours crowded into the front room to watch the ceremonies being relayed from the capital, on a tiny Bush television.

The Queen's first state tour of Scotland came just weeks after Elizabeth was crowned Queen on 2 June, 1953. The seven-day tour, which included appearances in Glasgow, Edinburgh and Coatbridge, was a resounding success. In this photograph there is no room in Coatbridge as everybody tries to see Queen as the Royal convoy passes through. People jammed the town, packed the streets, stood on balconies, went up on roofs, clung to flagpoles and stood on chairs to get a better view. In the image above we can see a smiling Queen in Ballater Street, Gorbals, with Lord Provost Mrs Jean Roberts. Residents had waited for hours to get a chance to see the Royal visitor. Arms were raised and flags waived as a relaxed Queen Elizabeth made light of her busy schedule. The main event had taken place at Hampden Park on 25 June, 1953, when Royal fever swept the city. More than 60,000 enthusiastic people gathered in sweltering sunshine to honour the Queen and Prince Philip.

Did you know?

Hampden Park holds the European record for attendance at a football match: 149,547 saw Scotland beat England 3-1 in 1937, in the days before leading British stadia became all-seated.

The Clyde is famous throughout the world for its shipbuilding. It has been called the cradle of steam navigation and is the birthplace of the Queen Mary and countless other liners, warships and cargo ships.This photograph shows the debut of RMS Queen Mary, after leaving the confines of the shipyard for the first time on 24 March, 1936, as it sailed out of the Clyde as far as Arran for preliminary trials. Construction on the ship, then known only as "Hull Number 534", began in December 1930 on the River Clyde by the John Brown & Company shipbuilding and engineering shipyard at Clydebank. The Company built many notable and world-famous ships and at its height, from 1900 to the 1950s, it was one of the most highly regarded, and internationally famous, shipbuilding companies on the planet. It carried a strong reputation for building reliable passenger vessels, many for the Cunard line. The ship was named after Queen Mary, consort of King George V. Until her launch the name she was to be given was kept a closely guarded secret. The world's greatest liner was launched by Her Majesty at

Clydebank on September 1934. During the Second World War, Queen Mary was the largest and fastest troopship involved in the war, frequently carrying as many as 15,000 men in a single voyage, and often travelling out of convoy and without escort. The Queen Mary was retired from service in 1967 after she had completed her 1,000th and last crossing of the North Atlantic. It had sailed more than 5.6million nautical miles - and carried 2.5m passengers. After her retirement she steamed to Long Beach, California, where she is permanently moored as a tourist attraction, hotel, museum, and event facility.

Did you know?

The world's last sea-going paddle-steamer, the 'Waverley', was built on the banks of the River Kelvin by A & J Inglis in 1947.

The main aerial photograph gives you some idea of the scale of the project. Much of the event was located on a 120 acre site which had been created in the eastern part of Prince's Dock on the south bank of the River Clyde at Plantation Quay, in Govan. Two special feature areas were created: the High Street, which was decorated with outlines of Glasgow's best known spires and towers, containing more than twenty single storey shops, and Bell's Bridge, installed to provide access from the opposite bank of the river. Special features also included the 240 feet (73m) high Clydesdale Bank 150th Anniversary Tower, the Coca-Cola Roller roller coaster, a miniature railway and five former Glasgow Corporation Tramways vintage trams running again in the city along the riverside.

Don't start thinking you have had a wee dram too many, because this gentleman sitting in Glasgow's Central Station, actually has been photographed with a plant pot on his head. He has presumably been strategically placed to advertise the event held in 1988. It was the first event of its type to be held in the city in 50 years, since the Empire Exhibition of 1938. It attracted 4.3 million visitors over 152 days, by far the most successful of the five National Garden Festivals held throughout the UK. The official opening ceremony took place on 29 April and was conducted by Prince Charles and Princess Diana.

A bleak and watery picture from January 1968, as bare-footed shopkeepers try to clear as much of the flood water as they can from the premises on the corner of Garry Street and Holmlea Road, in the Cathcart area of Glasgow. The devastation was caused when Hurricane Low Q moved through the Central Belt of Scotland during mid January. It arrived with almost no warning and left behind a trail of destruction. Winds of up to 110mph tore through Glasgow causing roofs to fall apart and chimney heads to come crashing through tenement flats. Streets were covered in rubble and cars crushed under masonry. It is reported that in Glasgow alone, over 300 houses were destroyed and 70,000 homes were damaged. Many people evacuated the then Europe's tallest flats as they began swaying. After the storm moved away,

the clean-up operation began. An interest-free loan of £500,000 was given by the Labour Government to the affected areas. Singer Frankie Vaughan began to raise funds for the victims of the storm by holding a special concert at the Alhambra Theatre in Glasgow.

> ## Did you know?
>
> *The original underground system was cable operated was the world's third underground railway.*

On the left we can see that the The Queen Mother, looking resplendent in her cream coloured coat and hat, is ready to cut the tape to open the new Kingston Bridge in Glasgow. Built between 1967 and 1970 at a cost of £11 million, the ten-lane Kingston Bridge links the eastern and western sections of the M8 motorway, crossing the River Clyde in the centre of the city of Glasgow. In 1967 work began on the Kingston Bridge which was the second longest spanning pre-stressed concrete bridge in Britain. It was opened in June 1970 by the Queen Mother and continues to carry traffic on what is, at peak hours, one of the busiest sections of road in Europe.

The Pope's visit to Britain in 1982 drew huge crowds wherever he went and was the first visit by a reigning pontif. During his time in the UK the visit included nine cities, delivering 16 major addresses. On a swelteringly hot day in June, 300,000 people - the biggest crowd ever assembled in Scotland - gathered at Glasgow's Bellahouston Park to attend Mass celebrated by John Paul II. The pope travelled by helicopter to the event but the masses had to travel by road, and this image gives a small hint of the unparalleled level of congestion. Applause for the Pope lasted for seven minutes when he tried to address the congregation, which was shepherded by 7,000 stewards and 6,000 police. The following day included a visit to patients at St Joseph's Hospital in Rosewell and an address at the former priests' training centre St Andrew's College.

GETTING AROUND GLASGOW

To the left is a splendid nostalgic view of Parkhead Cross in the East End of the city taken from the entrance to Burgher Street on Tollcross Road. The heavy and diverse traffic shows what an important junction it was at the time. The policeman in the centre of the road looks in a very precarious position, as traffic of all shapes and sizes passes him on all sides. Looking ahead we can continue along to Gallowgate or turn right into Duke Street. Immediately to the right we can see the point where Westmuir Street joins the Edwardian five-way junction. Several fine buildings making the junction notable, such as the former Glasgow Savings Bank. The junction can become even busier due to match day traffic for football games at nearby Celtic Park. In recent years the area around this historic junction has been part of regeneration plans and awarded £1.7m by the Heritage Lottery Fund.

The gentleman above looks as though he may get rather wet as he sits outside the Kings Theatre in his elegant open-top Wolseley motor car. The King's Theatre occupies the corner of Bath Street and Elmbank Street, in the Charing Cross area of the city. One of Scotland's most historic and significant theatres, The King's opened in 1904. This gentleman was proud to be waiting in his new Wolseley, possibly to pick up one of the female theatre cast. Brilliantly designed by prolific theatre architect Frank Matcham it has played host to top stars and shows ever since. The theatre was primarily a receiving house for touring musicals, dance, comedy and circus-type performances. The legendary Half Past Eight Shows ran for 26 weeks a season. Back in the day, Wolseley made a serious bid to become a true mass-producer of popular cars but faced stiff competition from Morris, Austin, Singer and Rover.

These images from the turn of the last century, show part of the St Enoch Hotel and Railway Station, the entrance to the St. Enoch Subway Station and the St Enoch Hotel in addition to another notable landmark at the time, St. Enoch Church in the bottom picture. They give a nostalgic view of what was once a thriving transport hub. The station opened in 1876 and the hotel followed three years later. It had 12 platforms, covered by a glass arched roof and serving over 23,000 passengers a day. At the time, it was described as "the most imposing structure in Glasgow" and with over 200 bedrooms, made it the city's largest hotel. Both the station and the hotel were among the first buildings in Glasgow to be lit by electricity. Sadly, it closed in 1966 following the renationalisation of the railways, with services being diverted to nearby Glasgow Central. Today, only the

Subway building survives, the church was unfortunately swept away in 1926 and the hotel which fronted the station, was demolished in 1977. On the site now is another glass structure, the St. Enoch Centre shopping mall, with the former St Enoch Subway station now converted into a café.

The Working Class children of the late Forties early Fifties were not a generation that was used to being passively entertained on a daily basis. Most working class homes back in the early Fifties did not have a TV and they were left pretty much to make their own entertainment, which they did quite well. One very popular hobby for young boys was train-spotting. The lads in this photograph have been waiting patiently for this steam train to arrive at St Enoch's Station, in 1957. During the long summer holidays it was great to set off on a days trainspotting with a supply of jam sandwiches and lemonade. Next best thing was playing with a Hornby train set, which comprised of a circular track, an engine and some wagons. In many cases, this began a love affair with trains that lasted well into adulthood.

The Renfrew Ferry crosses the Clyde between Renfrew and Yoker. The original service operated further upstream from a spot close to where the Braehead Shopping Centre now stands, but moved here in the early 19th century. Tunnels and bridges came to replace many of the ferries that plied a trade across the river, but the terrain here makes such building work difficult and expensive to carry out. So, Renfrew Ferry continues to be in use today. It was a foot passenger only enterprise until after the last war, but offered a ferry service for motor vehicles as car ownership blossomed. However, the opening of the Clyde Tunnel saw business drop off and it reverted to serving pedestrians in 1984. One of the old ferries is now a nightspot, moored at Broomielaw.

No, this is not some form of 1927 ducking stool. It was the trolley chair used by locals to cross the River Cart, a tributary of the Clyde that joins this river midway between Erskine and Renfrew. It can be a safe bet that the woman being winched across the water was not of a mind to upset the one turning the handle. If she had anything to say, it was a good idea to keep it to herself until she was on dry land! Another good reason to stay out of the water was that some of Paisley's sewage used to find its way into the Cart.

Springburn is a district on the northern side of Glasgow. Here we are looking back along the road towards the city centre. Originally a rural hamlet, as industrialisation came to the area it was incorporated into Glasgow Corporation in 1872. Springburn's economy was largely linked with locomotive manufacture and four large sites were based in the vicinity around the turn into the 20th century. Sadly, in recent times, Springburn has gained an unwelcome reputation because of social problems that have led to it being regarded as one of the country's most feared neighbourhoods. It can, though, boast to being the birthplace of some who achieved fame elsewhere. They include singer Karl Denver, footballer Mo Johnston and Dr Who actor Peter Capaldi.

The Charing Cross of the middle years of the last century looks significantly different from the modern scene that is now dominated by the long, penetrating finger of the M8 motorway. In the scene we have here, the Grand Hotel dominates the left hand side of the picture. Many famous and titled people have passed through its doors, including the Prince of Wales who stayed here in 1888 before attending the International Exhibition at Kelvingrove. In the centre, further down, we can identify the impressive Charing Cross Mansions under their decorative cupola. The delightful tenement block was built in 1891 for the warehousemen Robert Simpson & Sons and is a distinctive landmark, with its ornate clock and carved figures. The water fountain, on the left, is still on the corner with Woodside Crescent, but the Clydesdale Bank has replaced the hotel that was demolished over 40 years ago.

Some readers may remember the major reorganisation of traffic at Eglinton Toll in 1946, including the erection of a barrier separating traffic flows along Victoria Road from those in Pollokshaws Road. The photograph is taken from an elevated view in the tenement building looking towards Queen's Park. McNee's pub is visible on the left, with the Plaza dance hall nearby and further up Butterbiggins Road. The tramcars carefully make their way through the track relaying work and pass only inches away from the workmen. These four-wheeled, double-deck tramcars were the mainstay of the Glasgow tram fleet from electrification until the late 1950s. Tramcar 853, on the right, was the second last to retain the green route colour in 1943.

Did you know?

Glasgow, with a population of around 600,000, is Scotland's largest city and is the commercial capital of Scotland. It is the UK's largest retail centre after London.

Glaswegians turned out in their thousands to witness the closing procession of trams from the east end in an untimely deluge through the city centre and out to the South Side Car Works where most would be scrapped. It was over half a century ago, but for many people who remember the last tram procession which took place in Glasgow on 4 September, 1962, it was like it was yesterday. Twenty iconic trams from the last 90 years of city history took part in the route, led by a horse drawn tram from 1894 (see picture). They glided over rails through the city, winding from Dalmarnock tram depot in the east end through to the city centre and down Pollokshaws Road to Coplawhill tramworks, which is now the Tramway theatre. Over 250,000 people came out to say goodbye to the trams, some from other parts of the UK. The Coronation Tram was the very last tram in the procession that night and many folk put a penny on the tram track as a souvenir to get it squashed to keep as a momento. The trams had been slowly withdrawn from Glasgow life for many years and just before the procession, the only route running in the city was the number nine from Auchenshuggle to Dalmuir. From a maximum of more than 1,200 trams in 1947, the system was gradually wound down from about 1953 onwards. Glasgow was a great tramway city and was the last in the UK to survive, apart from the Blackpool coastal tramway, which caused people to travel the length of the country to get a last lingering look of the unique closing procession.

Did you know?

The word 'Glaswegian' is thought to have been introduced in 1817 by Sir Walter Scott.

The war was over and some semblance of normality had returned to Buchanan Street, looking north along it from Argyle Street in 1946. The sight of horse drawn vehicles rolled back the years for those who remembered when the noble steed dominated the highways at the beginning of the century, pulling wagons, trams, carts and carriages. But it was not a nostalgic longing for the old days that brought Dobbin out of retirement, it was something of a necessity as petrol and diesel supplies were scarce. Rather than give up the ghost, some traders and travellers turned back the clock and Buchanan Street echoed to the sound of clip-clopping hooves once again. As the horses moved away from the city centre gardeners living in the outskirts were glad to see them pass by for, armed with bucket and shovel, there was an instant source of fertiliser for the rhubarb readily available. Out of town it was still a common sight to see the rag and bone men with their horses and carts even in the 1950s. Just like Steptoe and Son, with their loyal servant Hercules between the shafts, they toured the streets, riding a version of side saddle on their carts as their legs dangled over the sides, calling out to housewives to bring their unwanted junk into the street. This was recycling in its crudest form, but families were happy to make an exchange of cast offs for something with which to donkeystone the front step.

Below we can see that queue's have started to build at Glasgow Central Station as thousands of Glaswegians make a break for the coast... the Wakes holidays are about to start in 1959. Workers rushed home to get ready for a Friday get away before the real crowds build up on Fair Saturday. The Clyde coast, Largs and Fairlie will be popular destinations. More intrepid souls would venture further afield to Blackpool and the Isle of Man. Even Spain could be on the horizon as this was the start of the package holiday boom. We can see from the book stall clock it is almost 6.30pm and a long line of travellers is already building at the platform entrance. The station has been refurbished in recent years but it still retains some of the more endearing original features. As you walk through the station you can't help but notice the old world charm and the vast expanses of wrought iron work.

Did you know?

The story of Percy Pilcher who lived in Byres Road, Glasgow and was 4 years ahead of the Wright Brothers in constructing and testing gliders, but met his untimely death in a flying accident.

In this busy Glasgow street scene, a man and young schoolboy seem to be taking their life in their hands, crossing the busy main road packed with traffic. Trams, lorries, cars and even fire engines can be seen in this small area of cobbled road. Maybe the fire engines are there because of an incident that has caused the log jam, or perhaps its just the normal lunchtime traffic in the centre of a city the size of Glasgow. With the traffic not moving the trams have stacked up in a row one after another and the passengers are probably in for a long wait. This looks like Argyle Street with Lewis's store on the right of picture. Lewis's opened in 1929 and boasted seven selling floors and was not to be mistaken for John Lewis. At the time, Lewis's Glasgow was one of the largest department stores in the UK. Some older readers may well have worked in the store as it employed nearly 1400 staff by the late 1970s. Children of the early 1980s ultimately were the last to experience its famous Santa's Grotto and massive toy department on the fifth floor, not to mention the amazing foodhall on the ground floor. Such was the popularity of the store that despite Debenhams taking over the reins in 1990, Glaswegians still refer to the building as Lewis's.

The Carnival has a long association with Glasgow Green and between early June until the end of August the cacophony of noise would build with screaming of girls on the fairground rides, the loud music and the noise from the large engines that powered the different rides and attractions. The young girls in this photograph are enjoying the thrill of the chair swing ride, and in the background, young and old can have a turn on the Helter Skelter ride. Users of the wooden construction ride would climb up inside the tower and slide down the outside, usually on a mat or hessian sack.

ENTERTAINMENT, LEISURE & PASTIMES

All the fun of the Fair!!..to be precise the 'Carnival'. On this page, we have two images from Vinegar Hill around 100 years ago. The boys and girls are enjoying the thrill of the swingboat ride in the top picture. In the image to the right, crowds flock to the crowded pitch with its blaring merry-go-rounds and Clarke's thrilling ghost illusion, in those days a household name throughout the length and breadth of Scotland. We can see that in the Edwardian age it was fashion for everyone to wear a hat. It did not matter if you were poor or rich, old or a child, whatever the status a person wore a hat. They obviously believed in the old saying, 'if you want to get ahead and get noticed, then get a hat'.

Vinegarhill became the prime site in Glasgow for the annual carnival, and the show folk were to have along association with Camlachie. The 'shows' were located on the north side of Gallowgate, on both the east and west sides of Vinegarhill Street. John Manders moving wax-work was always strongly patronised. Professor Anderton's flying bird cage created a great sensation, while another attraction was John Swallow's popular Circus. There was something to suit every taste in the grounds. Vinegar Hill of today gives little or no indication of the attractions which made it a Mecca of amusement-seekers.

A very wintry scene shows a large number of Greenock residents enjoying themselves in the snow in 1947. On 4–5 March came one of the worst British blizzards of the 20th century, which left drifts across much of the country with some lying 7 metres (23 ft) deep in the Scottish Highlands. In some places snow fell on 26 days out of 28 in the month. Despite the fact that people were out enjoying themselves, cold weather exacerbated the fuel problem. Stockpiles of coal at the pits and depots froze solid and could not be moved. Fuel supplies remained insufficient and blackouts occurred across large swathes of the country, with even the staff at Buckingham Palace, the Houses of Parliament and London's Central Electricity Board apparently reduced to working by candlelight. Despite the hardships, people were out to enjoy the winter sports conditions on Lyle Hill, with children and adults alike taking the chance to sledge down the steep slope.

Is this how Tom Daley started, I wonder? More likely just a group of guys showing off by diving into the cold and salty water at Gourock's outdoor swimming pool, right. The possibility of changing weather adds drama to the view from the poolside, out across the Clyde to Loch Long and beyond. The location is not just for show though, as the water that fills the pool is actually taken from the Clyde itself. The original pool opened in 1909 and today, is one of only two heated outdoor pools left in Scotland. Recently refurbished as part of a £1.8m renovation project, the pool offers a taste of the past in modern surroundings. Things have changed from yesteryear, however, as now you can participate in a number of organised activities at the pool, including a midnight swim.

© courtesy of Herald and Times Group

Pictured hanging on for dear life on the left is two and a half year old Joyce McChlery, as this male, probably dad, goes skating down Bingham's Pond in 1958. The pond can be found on the A82, Great Western Road, Hyndland, approximately 3 miles north west of the city centre. It was created in the 1880s on the site of old brick and coal pits. It was originally designed as a skating pond, and was the first home of Glasgow Curling Club, founded in 1830. A cold snap each year meant the water froze and became a firm favourite with locals, who took the opportunity to get out the old skates and get on the ice. Obviously, the depth of the ice was not so much of a health and safety risk in those days and the locals enjoyed the recreation on the community pond. Friends and neighbours would even get out and clear snow to make their own curling rink.

© courtesy of Herald and Times Group

With a black cab on every street corner, the Glasgow Taxis brand is a familiar one on city streets, but not very often will you see a line of 120 black cabs on a long winding trail in the countryside. This photograph was taken in 1955 as part of the Fund for Sick Children Outing which has been run since 1945. We can see the unusual sight of some of the taxis decorated with streamers and bunting, taking children from Mearnskirk Hospital on their annual outing. This famous childrens day out started by just three Glasgow taxi drivers and today involves around 150 cabs taking upwards of 400 children with special needs on a festive parade to Troon. Mearnskirk Hospital, in Renfrewshire, opened in 1930 and was originally built as a tuberculosis hospital for children by Glasgow Corporation's Public Health Department. The hospital, which was sited in the countryside away from the pollution of the city, was built on the the land of the old estate of Southfield.

those famous words, 'Are you dancin'?'. The ballroom was named for Prince Albert and was originally the Warren Academy of Dancing, opened by John and Annie Warren. The Albert's popularity soared during the 1920s as the introduction of new risque dances like the Charleston brought more and more young Glaswegians flocking to the dance floor. It was said at the time that some young girls were only allowed to dance at the Albert because it was a reputable establishment where no drunks were allowed! The dance hall tradition remained strong in Glasgow for several decades. In the 1940s and 1950s, venues like the Plaza, the Barrowlands and Green's Playhouse seemed to be at the peak of their powers.

Would the lady above, and others like her, have been an inspiration to the likes of Olympic Gold Medalist, Rhona Martin, when she was growing up. This lady from Gatehouse of Fleet, is just taking her shot in the Curling Bonspiel in 1960. Traditionally, a Bonspiel would consist of several games, often held on a weekend. Prior to the twentieth century many were held outdoors on a frozen freshwater loch. Though not mandatory, curling teams involved in bonspiels often wear theme costumes. Today, almost all bonspiels are held indoors on specially prepared artificial ice. Curling became front page news in Scotland in 2002 when housewife and mother-of-two, Rhona Martin, became an Olympic legend by winning 'Gold' in Salt Lake City. The 35-year-old skip of Team GB's women curlers, delivered the nation's first gold medal at a Winter Games for 18 years, with the very last shot of a nerve-tingling final against Switzerland. Glasgow's own Lauren Gray was recently part of the Bronze Medal winning British team at the 2014 Winter Olympics in Sochi.

As we can see pictured right, ballroom dancing was a big part of life for many of us in the last century and Glasgwegians have always been known for their love of dancing. Glasgow's first dance hall, the Albert Ballroom on Bath Street, was opened in 1905, and it soon became Scotland's first ballroom to hold dances six nights a week. All good clean fun when couples got together with

It's amazing, these two women look like they are the negative and positive version of each other. They are showing us how the Twist should be danced, at the Dennistoun Palais. The well-dressed revellers were probably twisting away to a live band. Resident band, Lauri Blandford and his Orchestra, often stood aside for nationally-famous big bands such as the Joe Loss Orchestra. Swivelling the hips became a worldwide dance craze in the early 1960s. The Twist became extremely popular after Chubby Checker danced it while singing the song of the same name on the Dick Clark Show on 6 August, 1960. The song quickly hit number one on the charts and the dance swept around the world. As a dance craze it enjoyed immense popularity among young people and came under fire from critics who felt it was too provocative. In 1962, Chubby Checker's version of 'The Twist' again hit number one on Billboard's Hot 100 chart, becoming the second song to ever be number one on two separate occasions (Bing Crosby's 'White Christmas' was the first). The dance was so popular that it inspired additional new dances such as the Mashed Potato, the Swim, and the Funky Chicken.

This 1938 photograph, pictured below, shows the Roslea Drive entrance to Dennistoun Palais. The original 'Denny Pally' opened in 1922, but was destroyed by fire in 1936. When it was rebuilt and re-opened in 1938 it was the biggest dance hall in Glasgow, with a capacity of 1,800. It continued to provide memories for Glasgow dancers until the building was converted into a supermarket.

Just prior to its closure for major alterations in 1931, here we see massive queues outside the Coliseum for the opening night of one of Charlie Chaplin's greatest films, 'City Lights'. The Coliseum was built for the Moss Empire's theatre circuit and opened on 18 December, 1905. It was designed by the most prolific UK theatre architect Frank Matcham. It began cinema use from 1925 when it was sold to the ABC, and in 1929 was the first cinema in Glasgow to screen 'talkies' when Al Jolson in 'The Jazz Singer' played here. In 1962, the front of the top balcony was partially removed to allow for the installation of Cinerama, as can be seen in the photograph above. This was designed by architect Leslie C. Norton. The first programme in Cinerama was 'How the West Was Won'. The building was closed in 1980 as the result of a Compulsory Purchase Order. In June 1986, Historic Scotland designated the Coliseum Cinema a Grade B listed building. After a number of years as a Bingo hall the building finally closed in 2003. The building remained empty and unused until a major fire caused it to be demolished in June 2009.

Did you know?

Did you know that Stan Laurel made his first stage appearance at a Glasgow Music hall? It was the Britannia, which was renamed the Panopticon by A.E. Pickard.

On the left crowds have started to gather as the trick cyclist on stilts stops Glasgow tram No 224 on its way from Mosspark to Pollokshields. He can be seen leaning against the tram advertising Billy Smarts Circus in this 1954 image. Billy Smart founded his circus in 1946 and in the 50s and 60s a trip to the circus was still an eagerly anticipated treat for millions of British schoolchildren. His Circus became a household name at the time, through the quality and slickness of its touring productions.

The standard four-wheeled, double-deck tramcars were the mainstay of the Glasgow tram fleet from electrification until the late 1950s (due to the imminent closure of the system).The tram system was gradually phased out between 1956 and 1962 (in favour of diesel-powered buses), with the final trams operating on 4 September, 1962. Apart from the Blackpool tramway, Glasgow became the last place in the UK to operate trams until the opening of the Manchester Metrolink in 1992.

Now, there's posh. Three generations of one family watch the small screen intently on 23 December, 1949. Goodness, at that time, most people could not afford a radiogram, never mind a television. It would not be long though, before this luxury became an essential part of family entertainment. Until then, an invitation to watch a programme on someone's private set was a privilege. It was the 1953 Coronation that helped promote the invasion of the goggle box into all our lives. People with TVs suddenly discovered that they were the most popular neighbours in the street as locals with whom they had seldom shared a conversation were able to negotiate an invite into the front room. After enjoying the entertainment offered by the splendour of the wedding coach on its way to Westminster, dads were instructed to put television high on the list of goods that they could get on hire purchase. To modern youth the tiny screens and fuzzy pictures would seem hilarious.

Happy summer scenes of a crowded beach in Rothesay in its heyday, in 1955. During the Victorian era, Rothesay developed as a popular tourist destination. It became hugely popular with Glaswegians going "doon the watter" and can be reached by ferry from Wemyss Bay which offers an onward rail link to Glasgow. Ettrick Bay was the most popular of all the bays which from the island's coastline. Its long stretch of

The first modern two-piece costume was created by Louis Reard in 1946, naming it the 'bikini' after the atoll where atomic bomb test were being carried out. Reard reasoned that the costume's effects would be akin to that of a nuclear reaction and he was not far wrong. With all the sea air and sunshine, some of the older ones took the opportunity to take a quick nap. The weather was irrelevant, what was important is getting away from work and the daily grind for a week.

sand and shallow water makes it an ideal place for the families on the beach. Scalpsie Bay is another very popular bay visited by hundreds daily.

Within a few years of these pictures being taken, many of the families pictured on the beach at Children's Corner would have been seduced by the promise of guaranteed sunshine and increasingly affordable package holidays to Spain. At the time these pictures were taken, you made your own entertainment if necessary and these women can be seen on beach the playing leapfrog. One woman may be asking the age old question, 'does my bum look big in this?', she is perhaps conscious of causing a stir with the menfolk on the beach. Her modern, knitted two-piece swimwear was designed to catch the eye rather than for practical purposes. Those who wore knitted costumes will remember with embarrassment how heavy and saggy they got when immersed in the sea.

As we can see competitors posing in their swimwear, line up for judging at Prestwick's open-air swimming pool in the 1950s. The hugely popular annual event, to crown Scotland's Seaside Queen, was watched by a large audience sitting in the sunshine around the pool side. Following World War II, beauty contests took place in a number of seaside resorts in Scotland, including Rothsay, Portobello, Dunbar and as seen here, in Prestwick. The events were a new kind of entertainment for the holidaymaker as the country moved on from the greyness and austerity of the war years. Fun for all the family; the men would enjoy watching pretty girls, the women would enjoy picking their favourites (and gossiping about the others), and little girls would dream of being bathing beauties when they grew up.

"I didn't get where I am today without being able to improvise" might be what this young cheeky girl on the left would say if she was asked about this photograph now. Despite the awful weather she has still managed a smile for the camera as she makes her way along the beach at Brodick, Isle of Arran. Not even the rain could dampen her fun as she used an inflatable dingy as a makeshift umbrella. At the time of this photograph in 1957, holidays abroad were still unheard of for most Glaswegians and the West Coast of Scotland provided happy holiday memories for many children and adults alike.

Taken in August 1936, this image shows children are taking advantage of a spell of sunshine by playing in the sand and paddling pool at Elder Park, in Govan. The 37 acre Elder Park was presented to the Borough of Govan in 1885 by Mrs Isabella Ure Elder in memory of her late husband, who had owned the shipbuilding yard that eventually became Fairfield's. As one of Glasgow's most scenic small parks, it opened in 1885 and for many years she paid for an annual display of fireworks there. Opening day was declared a public holiday and a parade marched from Paisley Road Toll to the park gates through streets decorated with flags and bunting. Now gone, the bandstand at Elder Park was a focal point for the local community.

In 1906 a statue of Isabella, in bronze on a granite base, was erected in Elder Park surrounded by a memorial garden. She is shown seated and wearing her academic gown. The sculptor was Glasgow graduate Archibald Macfarlane Shannan (1850-1915) and the £2,000 cost was raised by public subscription, much of it from the ordinary people of Govan who held her in high regard. It was the first statue of a woman (other than Queen Victoria in George Square) in the city and is still one of only three statues in Glasgow commemorating women. (The third is La Pasionaria on the Clydeside Walkway.) Isabella's statue is Category A listed and the monument and memorial gardens were restored in 2010.

Did you know?

The Western Baths - a private club - located in Cranworth Street is famed for the trapeze which spans the pool. It is also known for its occasional classical concerts held in the pool - when it has been emptied of water of course. Until the 1930 it had the biggest indoor pool in Scotland.

This splendid aerial shot of Hampden Park was taken during the 1954 meeting between Scotland and England, a game that was won 4-2 by the visiting team. The official attendance for the game was an enormous 134,544, the 5th largest for the Scotland National team in a home match. The record of 149,415 was against England at Hampden Park in 1937. Unusually, this game was both a Home Championship match and a World Cup - Group 3 qualifier. The massive crowd watched Scotland play well but lose the game, with the Scottish goals coming from Brown and Ormond. On a more positive note however, Scotland did qualify for the fifth World Cup Finals in Switzerland, after finishing runners-up to England in the group.

SOUTH EAST STAND

Located on Sauchiehall Street in Glasgow city centre, the building in these photographs has a long history of entertaining the public. It was built and opened in 1875 as the Diorama, became the Panorama in 1888, and altered in 1895 as the Ice Skating Palace. After further alterations in 1904 the

building became the Hippodrome and later that year it was taken over by Hengler's Circus. In 1927, after many years as a successful circus, it was largely rebuilt and converted to the Waldorf Dance Palace. Taken over by the ABC chain in 1929, they commissioned architect Charles J. McNair to alter the building into a flagship 'Super Cinema'. The Regal Cinema was opened on 13 November, 1929, with Al Jolson in 'The Singing Fool'. Seating was provided for 2,359 in stalls and circle levels. In October 1967, the Regal Cinema was re-named ABC 1, and a new construction was built adjacent on

the right-hand side of the building which contained ABC 2. In 1979, the two cinemas were rebuilt as the five-screen ABC Film Centre. It became the Cannon in 1986, and then MGM Cinemas following a fire in 1992. The complex had reverted to the name ABC Film Centre by the time of its closure in 1999. After sitting empty for several years, the large site has now been converted into pubs, restaurants and a music venue.

Glasgow Empire Theatre, known as the Glasgow Palace Empire until the early 1900s, was the major theatre in Glasgow, which opened in 1897 on the site of the Gaiety Theatre at 31-35 Sauchiehall Street. It was one of the leading theatres in the UK chain of theatres owned and developed by Moss Empires and became notorious within showbiz circles as 'The English comic's grave'. The theatre was designed by the renowned theatre architect Frank Matcham. Male impersonator, Vesta Tilley topped the opening bill.

The Empire presented variety, revues, musicals and dance, including Pavlova, winter circus, pantomimes and ice spectaculars. Over the years many stars appeared including Lilly Langtry, Laurel and Hardy, Sir Harry Lauder, the Logan family and Andy Stewart. Dance bands included Jack Hylton and Joe Loss. Top quality worldwide artistes were greatly welcomed, including Tony Bennett, Johnnie Ray, Frankie Laine, Connie Francis, Eartha Kitt, Howard Keel and Liberace were joined by Frank Sinatra, Dorothy Lamour, Bob Hope, Judy Garland, Jack Benny and a great favourite Danny Kaye.

Other performers from Britain who became regulars included Harry Secombe, Max Bygraves, Ken Dodd, Eddie Cochran, Adam Faith, Cliff Richard and Frankie Vaughan before he headlined at the Alhambra Theatre. Welsh singer Dame Shirley Bassey made her debut at the theatre in 1959 and was initially given a hard time before asking the audience to give her a chance, whereupon the singer finished her set and was warmly applauded. The final curtain came down on the theatre on 31 March, 1963, with a cast that included Duncan Macrae, Robert Wilson, Iain Cuthbertson, Albert Finney, Rikki Fulton and Andy Stewart. The site is now occupied by Empire House, an office and retail development.

BUILDINGS, MONUMENTS & BRIDGES

His Majesty King George, accompanied by the Queen, wait to lay the memorial stone of the new George V Bridge in 1927. This event took place a few months before the official opening of the bridge in 1928. The official in his full length ermine robe, was overshadowed by Queen Mary in a colourful patterned coat and hat. Their Majesties had a busy day in other parts of Glasgow, opening the new Kelvin Hall and placing a reef on the Cenotaph. The royal couple toured the city in an open backed limousine. The street was lined on both sides by soldiers holding rifles, with crowds waiting patiently behind them. The crowds wave flags and loudly cheer the royal couple.

In the photograph to the left we can see Lord Provost, Sir David Mason, leads official party across new King George V Bridge after opening ceremony in 1928. The three-arched road bridge was designed by Glasgow City Engineer, Thomas Somers, and links the southside Tradeston area to Oswald Street in the city centre. The bridge was commissioned in 1914, but was delayed due to the First World War. It is now protected as a Category B listed building. After the ribbon cutting ceremony, the photographer takes pictures of the large group as they cross the bridge.

Did you know?

In 1807 the Hunterian Art Gallery and Museum became the first public museum in Scotland.

On the left is a typical late 1920s street scene in Glasgow. Petrol engined vehicles were starting to emerge in greater numbers with the cars buses and lorries all parked on the road outside the Theatre Royal in Hope Street. The obligatory horse and cart travels up the road towards the junction at Cowcaddens Road and pedestrians without a care in the world take their life in their hands, by walking up the centre of the street. Glasgow Corporation Tramways (GCT) single-decker motorbuses were still largely seen as an experiment at the time. Not the most comfortable of rides, with their solid tyres and wooden seats. Opened by James Baylis in 1867 as the Royal Colosseum & Opera House, until changing its name to the Theatre Royal in 1869, The Theatre Royal is the city's longest serving theatre. In 1957 it became the Scottish Television Theatre, serving as TV studios for the newly formed STV. Throughout the years the Theatre Royal has had a firm place in the affections of theatre goers, not only in Glasgow but throughout Scotland. On its stage have appeared the cream of acting talent in theatre land.

first just a muddy hollow where horses were slaughtered. However, it was not long before handsome townhouses began to appear, along with a number of hotels.

The workman in the picture above is in a rather ungainly and precarious position as he and the statue of Prince Albert are lowered towards the plinth in the SW corner of George Square. The reason why it had been moved in the first place is unclear, but maybe after 60 years of bird droppings and sooty grime, it was time for a wash and brush up. Albert was the consort of Victoria, and he was present with the Queen on the visit made to Glasgow in 1849. Unlike Marochetti's earlier monument to Queen Victoria, this one to Prince Albert was commissioned after his death. Thousands of people came to the unveiling in 1866, and George Square was festooned with evergreens. The monument was well received, and in 1888 the Queen ordered a replica to be erected in Windsor Great Park.

George Square is notable for its many fine monuments and statues erected in the memory of some the city's favourite sons. They include Field Marshall Lord Clyde, Thomas Campbell, James Watt, Robert Burns, Sir Walter Scott and General Sir John Moore. The Square was named for King George III and laid out in 1781 as part of a central grid from Stockwell Street to Buchanan Street. This was largely based on plans by the architects known as the three James', Barry, Craig and Graham. It is difficult now to visualise that this spot was at

People look just like little ants, scurrying hither and thither, in this elevated 1937 shot of George Square looking across at the City Chambers. It is, perhaps, Glasgow's most impressive building, which is only fitting as it is the centre of local government and is its own monument to the power and wealth of the late Victorian era. Just as sumptuous inside as well as out, it was designed by William Young and has attracted visitors from all over the world since 1890. Two noble lions guard the white Cenotaph, unveiled in 1924 as a memorial to those who fell in the Great War. The single word 'pax' (peace), by the sculpted wreath and palm frond, makes the message simple and to the point. A multitude of monuments, statues and memorials to the great and the good abound in the square. The central column is topped by a statue to one of Scotland's foremost authors, Sir Walter Scott, creator of 'Rob Roy', 'Waverley' and 'Heart of Midlothian', amongst other notable works of the early 19th century. Scott was born in Edinburgh, but many of Glasgow's famous sons are remembered elsewhere around George Square. There are statues to Thomas Campbell, Lord Clyde, Thomas Graham and Sir John Moore, as well as those to 'foreign' politicians, royals and other important figures. In 1937, office workers in the City Chambers were taking a lunch break, enjoying the sunshine on the benches with their backs to the traffic, gazing across to the 1878 Post Office and the 1870 palatial building that now houses the tourist information centre.

The place where Jamaica Bridge spans the river has seen a number of structures built over the years to enable passage from one side to the other. One of the most significant should have been the one designed by the legendary Thomas Telford. Built in 1833, replacing the 1777 bridge, it did not see out the century. Found to be too narrow to accommodate the volume of traffic using its carriageway, the supporting arches were too close together to permit the passage of large vessels. The current bridge, remodelled in the 1890s, retained many of Telford's granite facings, balustrades and copings. The bridge is also known as Glasgow Bridge and was called Broomielaw Bridge in earlier times. The trams are running along part of the original route between St George's Cross and Eglington Toll that opened in 1872.

There are peaceful green parts to every city, though it is sometimes hard to appreciate they exist when battling with crowds of commuters in the busy centre. In 1936 this view of Glasgow University, with the Kelvingrove Art Gallery and Museum to the left, was taken from Park Terrace, where grand houses have curved away majestically since 1855. The university is one of Britain's oldest, having been established in 1451 in the cathedral by Bishop William Turnbull, with the blessing of an edict from Pope Nicholas V. The seat of learning soon moved to High Street, where it continued until the poor condition of the buildings forced relocation to Gilmorehill in 1864. The resplendent tower was the brainchild of that remarkable and prolific Victorian architect, Sir George Gilbert Scott. He restored such famous monuments as Ely, Salisbury and Lichfield cathedrals, as well as Westminster Abbey. The art gallery and museum building was the centrepiece of the 1901 Exhibition that marked the 50th anniversary of the Great Exhibition at the Crystal Palace, London. Its fairytale towers, spires and turrets lend an air of make believe to its architecture that has attracted local inhabitants to it for over a century.

The pair of handsome stone lions, designed by Ernest Gillick, guard the Cenotaph near the entrance to the City Chambers municipal buildings. The truncated granite obelisk, a monument to those who fell in the Great War, was created by JJ Burnet and stands some 30 feet high. It has a gilded metal cross in the form of a sword above an image of St Mungo. The Cenotaph was unveiled in 1924 by Earl Haig, the wartime Commander of the British Expeditionary Force (1915-18). The City Chambers were opened by Queen Victoria in August 1888, though the first council meeting was not held there until over a year later. The handsome edifice was built to a design drawn by William Young, a native of Paisley.

You could almost be in old Athens or ancient Rome when looking at the magnificence of the architecture that produced the Royal Exchange, though the road setts, street lamps and overhead wires might spoil the illusion. Despite that, it can be appreciated as an outstanding example of Georgian work that was built in 1780 for William Cunninghame, an immensely rich tobacco merchant who paid the then mammoth sum of £10,000 for its construction. The Royal Bank of Scotland bought the mansion in 1817 and Royal Exchange Square developed around this building from 1827, when it became the centre for trading tobacco, rum and sugar. As the industrial revolution took hold, iron, coal and shipping became incorporated into its dealings. The Royal Exchange flourished for over a century before the council used it to accommodate Stirling's Library in 1949. In 1996, it was transformed into the Gallery of Modern Art and the floor where traders used to barter is now called the Earth Gallery, displaying the work of some postwar Scottish artists, for example Howson, Currie and Campbell. The mounted figure outside the old Exchange is a representation of the victor at Waterloo, Arthur Wellesley, Duke of Wellington. It was erected in 1844 and is one of many examples of the Victorians' fascination with military might as they put up countless statues and named hosts of streets after Nelson, Wellington, Garnet, Gordon and other commanders.

Here is a rare and nostalgic view along High Street, Paisley from around 65 years ago. A very different age with tramlines down the centre and a distinct lack of traffic on the roads. To the left is Storrie Street, and in the distance is Thomas Coats Memorial Church which has been part of the Paisley sky-line for more than a 100 years and is sometimes called the Baptist Cathedral of Europe. The building, in red sandstone, is Gothic in design by Hippolyte Jean Blanc, topped with a crown spire rising to more than 60 metres above ground-level and opened in 1894. On the right is Paisley Museum which opened in 1871. The building was designed by the well-known Glasgow architect John Honeyman and was paid for by Sir Peter Coats of the famous Coats thread manufacturing family. The museum and art gallery houses the world famous collection of Paisley shawls. The separate library building was added in 1901.

Did you know?

Glasgow Cathedral, also known as St Mungo's, is said to be on the site of St Mungo's church.

Here we have two views of Glasgow Cross and the Tollbooth Steeple. Glasgow Cross was an area where the first recognised centre of shopping was established and is one of the city's most historic sites. It is the meeting place for several important streets and has always been a busy and congested spot. In the 1960s picture above, taken from an aspect on Saltmarket, the Daimler buses were running on the No 37 route between Springburn and Castlemilk. The overhead wires were used by trolleybuses until they were withdrawn in 1966. The historic Tollbooth Steeple, on the left, dates from 1627 and was part of a larger building that housed the council hall, offices and gaol.

By May 1954, we had almost turned the corner of postwar austerity. The last remnants of wartime rationing had gone and we were starting to walk with a spring in our step, albeit a small one. The bobby on point duty in the middle of the junction at Custom House Quay had to keep his wits about him as traffic came at him from several directions at the same time. It would get more difficult as the years went by and the number of the cars on the road increased as the nation's economy took an upward swing. It has been a mix of dereliction and regeneration here over the intervening years since this elevated shot was taken. The suspension bridge across to the Gorbals was originally built in 1851-53 and reconstructed 20 years later.

Pictured left is a rather scary looking image from the late 1960s, as two scaffolders perch on a single girder almost 300 ft in the air (89 metres). These two daredevils were part of the construction team of the high-rise Red Road Flats, built between 1964 and 1969. Designed in 1962 by architect Sam Bunton for Glasgow Corporation, the flats were of unusual construction, being the only steel-framed high-rise structures in Glasgow, scheduled to house up to 4,700 people. Among the tallest buildings in the city, views from the top draw the eye along the Campsie Fells to Ben Lomond and the Arrochar Alps, then west past the Erskine Bridge and out to Goat Fell on the Isle of Arran continuing south over Glasgow and East towards Edinburgh. For most of the early residents, living in the flats meant a considerable and welcome rise in their living conditions, since most had previously lived in run-down housing, often severely overcrowded, either nearby or elsewhere in the city.

One person who was not put off by the height was French high wire artist Didier Pasquette. In July 2007, he undertook a high wire stunt between two of the Red Road towers, attempting to cross the 150 ft gap between Towers 4 and 5. Although thwarted by Glasgow's temperamental weather he managed to walk 30 ft across the chasm, backwards on one occasion.

As we can see in the image below, difficult structural work is almost complete on the new Clydeside Expressway at Finnieston. Over 40 years old it has an interesting history and is a crucial piece of Glasgow's road network. The junction serves the area of Finnieston, the SECC, Glasgow Skypark and provides access to the Clyde Arc and the southside of the river and was one of the first to be constructed for the Expressway in 1971. It was an incredible technical challenge due to the requirement for the structure to pass over two abandoned railway lines.

GROWING UP IN GLASGOW

Here we have a scene of typical family life in the less affluent parts of Glasgow just after the last war, as many older readers will recall. The sight of so many women and children trying to enjoy a Sunday dinner in late 1947 is a poignant reminder of how difficult life was for many of us at that time. The tenement was an ideal way of housing a growing population, using the minimum of valuable building land. In the poorer areas some families lived in one or two-roomed flats. This is a George Street example of the smaller facility, known as a 'single-end'.

We have pleasure in featuring this photograph, below, from an age on innocence, when little girls were more than content playing with their little prams and dolls rather than their i-pads, i-phones and i-pods. Judging by the look on their little faces, taking 'dollie' out for a walk was a very serious business. The girls look like sisters and are extremely well turned out in their double-breasted coats and one has a very cute bow in her hair. Most girls would have a doll that they looked after as if it was a real baby. The dolls are being pushed along one of the paths in the Botanic Gardens and public park located in the West End of Glasgow, in 1957.

This happy-go-lucky gang of children had just been enjoying a game of street cricket in September 1956. It is not something you see much of today as youngsters are sitting in front of computer screens or fiddling with games consoles instead of getting out into the fresh air and making their own entertainment and socialising with their pals. These youngsters lived in the tenements at Govan, one of the working class districts on the banks of the Clyde that was once a major shipbuilding centre. Perhaps one of these kiddies had a younger brother called Kenny Dalglish or an older one who answered to the name of Alex Ferguson. Cricket is okay but they were probably just passing the time until the next game of footy!

On the facing page is a very poignant picture of the tenements era in 1950s Glasgow. This pair, probably brother and sister, have a playground which consists largely of cracked and broken concrete regularly flooded by broken down pipes. The only upside is that they are safe from the traffic in this backcourt, although mom is keeping an eye on them from the upper window, just to be sure. With few toys, children had to make their own amusement and these two had only one trike to share. In this instance, big brother is probably causing the wee lassie to have a glum face because he won't give her a turn. Wrapped up in her pinafore dress and oversized woolly jumper, she's heading off to explore pastures new. A few years after this picture was taken, the tenements of the old Gorbals were swept away along with many of the local communities.

Did you know?

Sir Thomas Lipton was born in Gorbals, Glasgow. He was known as 'The King's Grocer' and made his fortune mainly from tea and other enterprises.

Under the shadow of the christmas tree, left, a nurse at Yorkhill Children's Hospital tells one of her young patients the story of Christmas and Santa Claus. This type of work and kindness has been taking place at Yorkhill for a 100 years. In 1914, a major public appeal raised almost £140,000 to open the Royal Hospital for Sick Children on its current site at Yorkhill. The hospital was founded in 1882 and located in a house in Garnethill. It became apparent that the building was too small to meet the demand for its services and in July 1914 a new, purpose-built children's hospital was opened by King George V and Queen Mary on the site previously occupied by Yorkhill House. The hospital was designed by John James Burnet. Today, after the centenary celebrations have died down, the "Sick Kids" hospital with a worldwide reputation for excellence, is to move from its current site to the Southern General on the other side of the Clyde.

Traditional Scottish wear is for the whole family, not just for the adults, even the young ones can get involved. In the main extra cute photograph to the right, from December 1953, this wee laddie can be seen here rehearsing for his part as Harry Lauder, inset. Every child who attends the party at Bridgeton Day Nursery, near Glasgow, will have to do a turn at their Christmas Party. No doubt when he got a bit older, this young man would have been having a drink and singing along to some of Harry's favourite songs including; Roamin' in the Gloamin', I Love a Lassie, A Wee Deoch-an-Doris, and Keep Right on to the End of the Road, which is still used by Birmingham City Football Club as their club anthem.

Sir Harry Lauder, as he became, was once described by Sir Winston Churchill as "Scotland's greatest ever ambassador!" He was, at one time, the highest-paid performer in the world, reported to be making the equivalent of £12,700 a night plus expenses, and was the first British artiste to sell a million records. Lauder's music appealed to all, including workers, merchants, royalty, and presidents.

A group of children run towards the camera at Carmunnock Summer Camp in 1956. Carmunnock is 5 miles south of Glasgow and the kids at school called it 'the army camp'. The regime might have been quite tough but this was the only opportunity some of the children got to get away for a holiday. Away from the run down tenements and out in the fresh air of Lanarkshire these kids could have the time of their lives.

The best way to cool off in hot weather! These young children are posing for a photograph, hand-in-hand in the fountain at Butlins holiday camp, Ayr. It is hard to imagine that it was taken around 50 years ago when it was quite possible for Butlins to have up to 10,000 people staying on any one site and cheap package holidays where still to fully catch on. There's something very British about going on holiday to a windswept seaside resort, being woken up bright and early by loudspeaker announcements about vigorous exercise and enforced hilarity and then going back home a week later. The holiday camp, located near Ayr, originally opened in 1946 and contained all of the tried and tested Butlins ingredients. In the early days there was a very traditionally Scottish feel to the camp. Redcoats working here originally wore kilts and holiday makers also enjoyed a different kind of awakening. Instead of the early morning tune played by Radio Butlin, two pipers would solemnly march around the camp awakening every camper. In the 1950s, Des O'Connor first started entertaining people as a Butlins Redcoat at Ayr. Isla St Clair joined in 1969, followed by Russell Grant a year later. When this image was taken in the 1960s, full board would have been around £15 per week and the local resident band was Brian Poole and the Tremeloes, who had a No1 hit with 'Do You Love Me' in 1963.

Did you know?

The Boys' Brigade movement was started in Glasgow in 1883. It was started in Glasgow's west end by Sir William Alexander Smith and continued in that building for ninety years.

To the right, teeny-bopper fans go wild when the Bay City Rollers appear on stage in May 1977. At the peak of their popularity in the UK, comparisons were made to The Beatles. By early 1975, they were one of the highest-selling acts in the UK. A cover of the Four Seasons' "Bye, Bye, Baby" stayed at No. 1 in the UK for six weeks, selling nearly a million copies to become the biggest seller of the year, and the subsequent single "Give a Little Love" topped the charts that summer, their second No. 1 hit. For a relatively brief but fervent period (nicknamed "Rollermania"), they were worldwide teen idols. We can see by looking at this photograph, Bay City Roller fans in the mainly young female audience, had a completely distinctive style of dress, the main elements of which were calf-length tartan trousers and tartan scarves.'

Every country has their traditions and Scotland is no exception. As a child growing up one of the favourite customs was Guy Fawkes' Night or "Bonfire Night". In the days before and after Halloween people would make the effigy of Guy Fawkes, (an old cast-off jacket and trousers stuffed with straw or rags and newspapers and invariably a pumpkin head). This sextet of wee laddies probably didn't know Guy Fawkes from Guy Burgess, but that mattered little in the pursuit of some cash. They would wheel him around the neighbourhood in a pram or pushchair shouting "A Penny for the Guy", and try their 'butter wouldn't melt' charm to get mums and grandmas to open their purse strings. Who could resist the outstretched little hand and winning smile?! We were told the money they collected was to buy fireworks with, but more likely it was spent at the 'sweet shop' outside which the Guy was parked!

STARS SHINE IN OUR CITY

During Glasgow's industrial heyday many large firms held an annual sports day. The Singer factory sports day in Clydebank, was always highly regarded. On one very special occasion in the 1950s, captured below, the guest of honour was Hollywood film star Dorothy Lamour. She was probably best remembered for appearing in the "Road to"... movies, a series of successful comedies starring Bing Crosby and Bob Hope. In this glamourous and charming photograph she is seen flanked by two local girls, dressed up in elegant costumes for the occasion. Earlier, a cheering crowd of several thousand lined the barriers erected in Central Station when she arrived from London. She was escorted from the train to the Station Hotel and she exchanged greetings with some of her admirers.

Aww, bless his little cotton socks! This cute picture, right, shows two year old David Marshall from Dunoon shaking hands with the debonair and distinguished Cary Grant outside the Regal Cinema, Sauchiehall Street, in 1958. At this moment in time, Cary Grant was undoubtedly the world's favourite leading man – and was about to begin filming Alfred Hitchcock's 'North By Northwest'. In July 1958, the 54-year-old was promoting the film 'Indiscreet', in which he starred with Ingrid Bergman. By way of promoting his current film, he would come into the city, attend a preview which was then followed by questions from the audience. According to reports at the time, Grant's first stop in Scotland was in Lockerbie, where he supped ale and decided he'd like to eat fish and chips in the traditional fashion...with his fingers.

© courtesy of Herald and Times Group

A smiling Gene Kelly is seen here at the entrance to Glasgow Station. He was dressed for the Scottish weather, less than a year after he had made probably the most popular and admired of all film musicals – 'Singin' in the Rain'. After a period working in Europe for MGM, he returned to to Hollywood in 1953. The film musical was already beginning to feel the pressures from television, and it would appear as a result, MGM cut the budget for his next picture, 'Brigadoon', forcing the film to be made on studio backlots instead of on location in Scotland. He therefore decided to visit Glasgow on a research trip preparing for his role. The Cinemascope film version of 'Brigadoon', directed by Vincente Minnelli, was released by MGM in 1954 with Van Johnson and Cyd Charisse in leading roles alongside Gene Kelly.

Lulu is seen here signing autographs for a large crowd of fans, who have turned out the catch a glimpse of the Scottish star. She was born, Marie McDonald McLaughlin Lawrie, in 1948, in Lennoxtown, and grew up in Dennistoun, where she attended Thomson Street Primary School and Onslow Drive Junior School. She lived in Gallowgate for a while before moving to Garfield Street. At the age of 12 or 13, she and her manager approached a band called the Bellrocks seeking stage experience as a singer. She appeared with them every Saturday night. Lulu's big break came in 1964, after being signed by Decca their first single 'Shout' was a massive chart success.

Last minute queues at the end of the TB campaign in 1957 resulted in most of the stations remaining open well after the scheduled closing time of 10.00 p.m. The crowds were so voluminous that the police had to be called to keep order as the evening drew on. The George Square facility was open until midnight, the last X-ray being performed on Police Constable Robert Maxwell, aged 41. With the help of stars like Max Bygraves and other well known celebrities, along with a massive amount of work by everyone involved, astonishingly a total of 712,860 people had an X-ray during the five week period. In all, approximately 7,000 people had been found to be suffering from the disease, and the more serious cases were soon sent off to the allocated hospital beds for treatment. A fantastic campaign and a significant outcome for the people of Glasgow.

In the 1950s, the incidence of tuberculosis (TB) in Glasgow was higher than anywhere else in Europe and almost three times higher than in the rest of Britain. To combat this a campaign to eradicate the scourge of TB was launched in March 1957. A target of 250,000 X - ray examinations was set for the campaign. To be successful, every available means of publicity was employed in order to promote awareness of the operation.

One of the promotions to get people to turn up was the chance of winning a big prize. These ranged from an Austin A35 to a television set, a bathroom suite or a holiday in the Highlands. In the picture below Max Bygraves (who was appearing at the Glasgow Empire) can be seen presenting the prize of a washing machine to the lucky winners from Drumchapel. Max Bygraves had his own X-ray after the presentation.

A small group of exited female fans get a 'once in a lifetime' chance to meet 'The King' of rock 'n' roll. A rather bewildered Elvis got the surprise opportunity to meet his local fans at Prestwick airport in 1960 on his way home from doing his military service in Germany. During the short two hour refuelling stop, he can be seen here at the airport perimeter fence signing autographs and talking to the lucky few fans. Despite the information about his visit and flight being restricted, rumours that Elvis was arriving in Scotland soon leaked out. Many in the community were close to those who worked in the base, and a secret as massive as a visit by one of the biggest stars on the planet, was not something that was not easy to keep under wraps. For those in attendance this event was even more remarkable when you consider the status of such stars at the time, and the fact that this is thought to be his only officially recorded stop in the British Isles.

Above we see Muhammad Ali being given a traditional Scottish welcome as he stepped off the plane at Renfrew Airport in August 1965. His visit started on a positive note when Ali, formerly known as Cassius Clay, made a visit to Glasgow's Oakbank Hospital. He happily signed autographs and chatted to patients throughtout his visit. The fighter, then 23, also called in to Celtic Park before returning to his hotel. Boxing fans may remember his trip to Scotland for a different reason however. Reports from the exhibition match at Paisley Ice Rink the following night, suggest his pleasant demeanour disappeared. For some reason fans began booing during his exhibition bout against fellow American Jimmy Ellis. This did not go down well with the 'king of the ring' who marched out of the rink with his entourage and cancelled his hotel booking for the night, before demanding to fly out the same night.

Ken Dodd is pictured here in Bridgeton Child Welfare Clinic and Day Nursery, handing out vaccine impregnated sugar lumps to the children as part of Glasgow Corporation's Anti-Polio Campaign. Ken was taking time out from his part in that week's 'Startime' show at the Alhambra Theatre in April 1969. Ken helped to raise awareness amongst Glasgow mothers of the importance of immunisation against polio. He was happy to do anything he could to help protect the children against this terrible disease. Even today, Doddy and his famous tickling stick, travel the country virtually non-stop dispensing liberal doses of his unique tickle-tonic. He is currently celebrating nearly 60 years of happiness and laughter, having become a professional entertainer in 1954. Just a little over 10 years later, he made his debut at the famous London Palladium – where he enjoyed an unprecedented record breaking 42 week sell-out season!

Left is a fabulous picture of a relaxed and smiling Elizabeth Taylor in Royal Exchange Square, as she meets well-wishers after enjoying lunch at a Glasgow restaurant. The Hollywood movie star rounded off a holiday in Perthshire with lunch at Rogano on 4 September, 1979, before leaving for London. It is reported that a male fan heard she was dining there during her visit, and waited at the bar for five hours in order to present her with a bouquet of flowers, which she graciously accepted. Despite a colourful personal life, Elizabeth Taylor was the Queen of Hollywood, with a career spanning six decades. She had a special place in the hearts of a group of Celtic fans, who enjoyed a magical night in 1972 with the star and her then husband Richard Burton. Despite the loss to Upjest Dozsa the downhearted fans who headed back to the International Hotel to drown their sorrows were in for a surprise.

The generous Hollywood royalty were staying at the same hotel and spent the evening swilling Champagne and scoffing caviar with the football fans, soon taking their minds off the defeat.

Did you know?

The first teaching hospital in America, the Baltimore Infirmary, was founded by a Glasgow surgeon, Granville Sharp Pattison, in 1816.

THE WAR YEARS

During the last war there were frequent salvage drives. It was a waste not, want not culture and full of suggestions about making do and mending. Raw materials were scarce and anything that could be recycled was put to use. Those of us in the 21st century who think of ourselves as being 'green', and of being among the first to counteract the throwaway society, should look back to the 1940s. Here we can see that children collected all sorts of stuff that could be turned into something useful. Anything from an old envelope to a garden rail was collected and transported to a sorting centre.

In the late 1930s, as the outbreak of war seemed a certainty, civil defence groups began organising their strategies and trained members in the use of measures that would help combat the effects of modern warfare on the civilian population. The issuing of gas masks and instruction in their use was one such measure. All schoolchildren were issued with them in the early summer of 1939 and they carried them in purpose-built boxes to and from lessons. At the start of September 1939, any youngster being evacuated from the major urban areas clutched a battered suitcase in one hand and a gas mask in the other. Babies also had special helmets into which mothers would have to pump air with a bellows. Even the police were expected to don the less than flattering apparatus, but it was a wise precaution even if the fear of a gas attack never materialised.

There, armies of volunteers sifted and graded rags, bones, paper, metal and any other items that could be put to further use. Throughout the war years appeals for junk and salvage were ongoing. Sometimes we were asked to hand over old saucepans, flat irons and bedsteads to provide scrap metal for the building of new warships and planes. It seemed ironic that the Spitfire overhead might really be a flying frying pan. Not to worry, as long as it did its job. The British, weaned on a diet of jumble sales and white elephant stalls, were past masters (and mistresses) at scavenging. The skill was to serve them well.

The role of women in two world wars cannot be underestimated. The men departed in their millions, leaving behind factories, engineering works, farms and public transport vehicles without anyone to operate them. Step forward the fair sex. They tilled the fields and chopped down trees. Women handled heavy engineering plant and served in factories geared up for the war effort. They got behind the wheel of ambulances, tractors and trams and even took on new skills, such as servicing aeroplanes for the Royal Flying Corps. Towards the end of the war, those with a particular determination put on uniforms and joined the Women's Auxiliary Army Corps or Women's Royal Air Force. It was more of the same, but on a larger scale and with greater organisation, the second time round. When the balloon went up in 1939, there were already women's organisations officially in place.

Government figures show that women's employment increased during the Second World War from about 5 million in 1939 (26%) to just over 7.25 million in 1943 (36% of all women of working age). During WWII women worked in factories producing munitions, building ships, aeroplanes, in the auxiliary services as air-raid wardens, fire officers and evacuation officers, as drivers of fire engines, trains and trams, as conductors and as nurses. In this photograph we

can see women hard at work in the Rolls Royce factory at Hillington. Their efforts were critical to the war effort with the production of Rolls Royce Merlin engines for Spitfire fighters and Lancaster bombers. Peak production came in 1943, when 1,650 engines were dispatched in one month. Women played a vital part by 1941when they accounted for 41% of the total productive operators.

admirably portrayed by Bill Pertwee as Warden Hodges in the BBC sitcom 'Dad's Army'. During the blackout cries of 'Put that light out' and 'Don't you know there's a war on?' were often mimicked by comedians as part of their variety acts, but most wardens played an important role during the grim days of the early 1940s when we were under attack. They were often in the thick of it, assisting the general public find shelter during an air raid. They also reported the extent of bomb damage and assessed the local need for help from the emergency and rescue services. The wardens used their knowledge of their local areas to help find and reunite family members who had been separated during an air raid.

Stella, Lady Reading, founded her Women's Voluntary Service in 1938 and her members had already played their part in preparing the public for war on the home front with various civil defence training exercises. As men set off overseas, yet again women juggled home and family management with the demands of keeping the wheels of industry and food production turning. The Land Army was reformed in July 1939. Some 113,000 women, a third of all those employed in agricultural work, had done their bit in the service that was introduced in 1917. When peace was declared in 1945, there were 460,000 women in uniform and 6.5 million in civilian war work.

'What are you doing, mister?' This warden was using the telephone box as a handy resting spot as he filled out some return or checked a particular detail on his log of events. He was a member of the Air Raid Precautions (ARP) team of civilians who offered their services as volunteers on the home front. Many were in jobs that had a protected status as their work expertise was invaluable to wartime production. Others were too old or unfit to join up, but still wanted to play their part. There was also a small handful who just enjoyed being officious and belonged to what came to be known as the 'jobsworth' mentality. Such a type was

During World War II all sorts of essential and non-essential foods were rationed, as well as clothing, furniture and petrol. Before the Second World War started Britain imported about 55 million tons of food a year from other countries. After war was declared in September, 1939, the British government had to cut down on the amount of food it brought in from abroad and decided to introduce a system of rationing. People were encouraged to provide their own food at home. The 'Dig for Victory' campaign started in October, 1939, and called for every man and woman to keep an allotment. Lawns and flowerbeds were turned into vegetable gardens. Chickens, rabbits, goats and pigs were reared in town parks and gardens. Ration Books were issued to make sure everybody got a fair share. They contained coupons that had to be handed to the shop keepers every time rationed goods were bought. There was a shortage of materials to make clothes. People were also urged to 'Make do and mend' so that clothing factories and workers could be used to make items, such as parachutes and uniforms, needed in the battle against Germany. Every item of clothing was given a value in coupons. Each person was given 66 coupons to last them a year. Children were allocated an extra 10 clothing coupons above the

standard ration to allow for growing out of clothes during a year. This did not prevent children having to wear 'hand me downs' from older brothers and sisters. In a make do and mend environment, trousers and skirts were patched and darned, old jumpers were unpicked and the wool used to make new garments. Rationing continued even after the war ended. Fourteen years of austerity in Britain ended at midnight on 4 July, 1954, when restrictions on the sale and purchase of meat and bacon were lifted.

In those days unemployment benefit ran out after 26 weeks, leaving men totally bereft of financial means. Poverty went hand in hand with sickness and disease. This was a decade before the National Health Service was founded and doctors' bills were too much for ordinary folk. Many turned to quacks and self styled 'professors' of medicine who operated on street corners, travelling wagons or out of market stalls. This practitioner, looking like a cross between Ken Dodd and Max Wall, set himself up as a hair specialist. His potions for alopecia, dandruff and ringworm would have been largely ineffective as it was diet and housing conditions that were at the root cause of most people's problems.

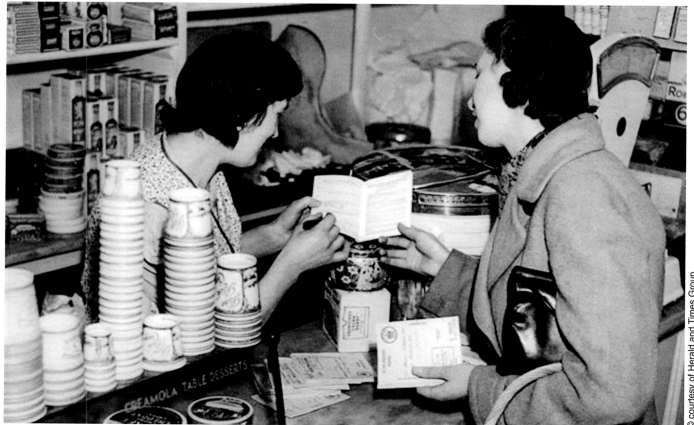

In the photograph below it looks like crowds have come out in force, to cheer on the brave volunteers of LDV on Kirkintilloch Road, Bishopbriggs. The name was changed from 'Local Defence Volunteers' to 'Home Guard' in July 1940 on the instructions of Winston Churchill as he felt that the original name was uninspiring. The LDV was open to men aged between 16 and 65 who had fired a rifle and were 'capable of free movement'. Neither of these qualifications was seriously tested. At first, there were rifles for only about a third of volunteers. The rest had to use shotguns, sporting rifles or 'weapons' such as golf clubs and broomsticks.

Perception of the Home Guard may have been distorted over the years, perhaps influenced by the popular TV comedy Dad's Army, but it appears the real truth about the Home Guard is very different, and this Dad's Army was very much a Lads' Army during the Second World War. RAF Bishopbriggs was a World War II barrage balloon depot, and the site of a large accommodation camp established as early as 1939.

Just to the north west of Stonehouse, Lanarkshire, lies wreckage on open moorland which led to one of the few unresolved mysteries of the Second World War. The wreckage was a Messerschmitt ME110 which had crashed shortly after the pilot, Rudolf Hess, had parachuted out. After his capture, over 70 years ago, he received a welcome perhaps less ebullient than he had expected, spending the rest of the war behind bars, including a brief stint as one of the last prisoners of the Tower of London. He undertook the solo flight in the belief he could arrange peace talks with the Duke of Hamilton, whom he believed was prominent in opposition to the British government. Few were sure whether Hitler's deputy had come with Hitler's backing but shortly afterwards German radio stations put out a message that Hess had been unwell and suffering from hallucinations. We can only speculate as to his actual motives.

It appears that the simplest and most plausible explanation is that the eccentric and unbalanced Hess, aware of his declining influence with Hitler, hoped to re-establish himself by a dramatic coup that would, he deludedly believed, bring peace with Britain and save Germany.

Did you know?

Glasgow had a professional Police Force before London? The Glasgow Police Force was formed in 1789, 40 years before the 'Peelers'.

This defused 1,000kg Luftmine was rendered safe on 18 March 1941. It was one of a contingent of heavy explosives that were dropped during a bombing raid on the city and fell to earth by parachute. Happily for us, this one did not go off but, of course, countless others did during enemy raids on our city. All such weapons are designed to create massive destruction, but those attached to parachutes were meant to act as blast bombs. They were supposed to detonate at roof level, thus maximising the aerodynamic effect of shock waves on whole streets rather than small clusters of houses. Popular singer, Al Bowlly, was killed in London by such a mine a mere month after the pictured one came to rest in Glasgow.

During World War II, the Glasgow Salvage Corps placed itself at the disposal of the city for firefighting duties. However, the salvage role was deemed more important and Corps members trained Fire Service members in salvage methods. The Auxiliary Fire Service had been formed in 1938, but all brigades were absorbed into the National Fire Service three years later. After the big air raids on Coventry and other English cities, Glasgow trained hard for what was, inevitably, to come its way. In September, 1940, bombs fell on Partick, Yoker and Yorkhill. A 250 lb bomb at Yorkhill quay hit the 10,000 ton cruiser Sussex and 2,000 residents were evacuated. However, this was nothing compared to the blitz on Clydeside in March 1941. Only a dozen houses escaped without damage. Further attacks during the year stretched the resources of the fire and salvage services. This two ton Austin K2 wagon, with its 30 ft ladder, was added to the fleet in 1942. It was used to pull various pumps, water tanks etc as and when required. The addition of radio communication in the cabs improved the speed and efficiency of reaction to any new incident. The badge of the Corps was displayed on its side. As well as the city coat of arms, the shield contained the wall, wave lines and flames. These represented the main elements of the salvage men's work. The wall was for protection, the wave lines for water and the flames for fire.

seam on the back of their legs to give the impression they were wearing nylons. There was a product on sale in chemists called "Leg-tan" but if you couldn't afford it, they used gravy browning powder, made in water as normal then applied to the legs and allowed to dry before the seam was drawn with eyebrow pencil, by another female. It was crucial to achieve knockout legs for that important dance.

This attitude went on to apply to everything and although they didn't use the term, reduce, reuse, recycle became the ethos of the times. People started making new clothes from old ones and from all other household linen. During the world wars women became masterminds of make do and mend, so resourceful they fashioned up sexy knickers out of parachutes. Making stuff was a way of life because daily necessities like clothes were not so readily available to buy.

The war effort wasn't all about scavenging metal for new war planes. There were any number of appeals for clothing and toys for displaced and unfortunate families. Here WVS members are surrounded with items collected or sent in to help those who were in need. The WVS became an official clothing distribution centre for Glasgow Corporation. The Post Office would provide the transport and delivery of the results of the appeal and the women would then leap into action. The dollies would bring joy to the hearts of little girls whose homes had been flattened by the 1941 Clydeside blitz and those of later Luftwaffe raids. The little lassie who would get one of these dolls as a gift to replace the one she had lost would gain much comfort from it. It would be something to cuddle and gain comfort from was.

Nylon stockings were a luxury item during WWII and as they were subject to rationing, quiet hard to get. They were very desirable however as it was very fashionable to wear them. As we can see in this photograph above, women often just drew a

SHOP 'TIL YOU DROP

The tramcar making its way along Union Street in 1947 belonged to the public transport vehicle service in which Glaswegians took great pride. It prospered during the reign of six monarchs and was a familiar sight on our streets for nearly a century. When this tram passed Boot's and Peacock's Tea Rooms and Restaurant, there were still some 1,200 'caurs' running in and around the city. The first route had opened in 1872, with horses providing the power to transport passengers along the tracks. An experimental electrified route between Springburn and Mitchell Street was begun in 1898. It proved to be a great success and horsepower was phased out by 1902. It was a sad day for traditionalists when the last tram took a final journey on 4 September, 1962.

Did you know?

The Bank of Scotland, founded in 1695, is the oldest surviving bank in the UK. It was also the first bank in Europe to print its own bank notes.

The Sancroft family, mother and sons, stand in the doorway of shop they opened as a newsagent and tobacconist, which was possibly run by the family over several generations. This is a typical example of a traditional tenement shop in the heart of Glasgow. Tobacco smoking was so much a way of life that there was no difficulty at all in finding somewhere to buy tobacco products. In particular there were showcases of them on public display for all to see. In the window we can see an advertisement for Mitchell's "Prize Crop" Cigarettes. The Mitchell family first established a tobacco manufacturing business in Linlithgow in 1723. The business transferred in 1825 to Candleriggs and several years later the business moved again, to St Andrew's Square. On his death, Stephen Mitchell left a public bequest of £66,998 10s 6d to ensure the establishment and maintenance of a public library in Glasgow, to be known as the Mitchell Library. The library was opened to the public in November 1877 and now we all recognise it as the largest public reference library in Europe.

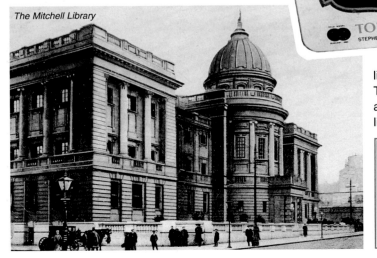

The Mitchell Library

Did you know?

The Mitchell Library is Europe's largest public reference library with more than a million volumes. It also houses the world's largest Robert Burns Collection.

96

Street in 1999. It has always been a classy part of the city and one that helped maintain that image by keeping such working class vehicles as trams away from its carriageway! Private, chauffeur driven limousines were fine, but those conveyors of the lower orders had to be redirected elsewhere, thank you very much.

Taking a close look at the image below we can just about see the elevated advert for Capstan cigarettes at the far end of the of Argyle Street, is a reminder of the days when smoking was an acceptable part of our daily life. It was not until 1965 that restrictions on promoting 'coffin nails' began to be seen to any degree when television advertising of such products was banned. In the past, this thoroughfare has had various names, including Dumbarton Road, Wester Gate and Anderson Walk. It settled on its present name in the memory of Archibald Campbell, the 3rd Duke of Argyll. A prominent Hanoverian politician, he was one of the Scottish peers chosen to sit in the first Parliament of Great Britain. He was also responsible for the rebuilding of Inverary Castle in 1743.

It has been some time since traffic moved along Buchanan Street. Back in the 1920s, this was a popular but free-moving part of the city centre. However, by the middle of the last century it was beginning to become congested, so it was no surprise to find it pedestrianised in more recent times. This helped confirm the area as one of Glasgow's premier shopping spots, especially after the opening of the Buchanan Galleries Centre at the junction with Sauchiehall

The lady at the front of the queue in this post war image, above, is looking to inspect the very small bird on offer at the mobile fish and poultry van on Dundas Street, Glasgow. It was a time when lives were starting to get back to some sort of normality. The fighting spirit that had kept the country battling on from 1939 to 1945 was all but gone a few years later, drained away for most people via a lack of everything: food, adequate housing, money and prospects. The only things in abundance were rationing coupons. Even when you did get your hands on a prized morsel, it was rarely a delicacy worth eating. Even the van has a wartime history, as it was formerly an RAF Ambulance.

It's clear to see from the image on the right from 1951 that Glasgow people were beginning to shop with more optimism after the devastation and resulting austerity of the war years. It is taken outside the original Marks & Spencer's store in Argyle Street. With Buchanan Street and Sauchiehall Street, Argyle Street forms the main shopping artery in the city centre. Crowds were out in force to grab a bargain for Christmas. Until recently, the area was characterised by four-storey sandstone tenements built at the end of the 19th century and the start of the 20th.

The long avenue of Sauchiehall Street stretches east from Charing Cross. The Coronation trams, a permanent feature on Glasgow's streets in 1938, were a new line, having replaced the older and less reliable Standards. Making their way towards the Grand Hotel, from where this photograph was taken, passengers might have been getting off at the corner on the right. If so, it could have been to pay a visit to William Skinner's Tea Rooms. Skinner's was just one of a number of such fashionable places to take light refreshment in the middle of a shopping spree. Cranston's and Craig's were rivals who also offered a good standard of service. Sauchiehall Street was always noted for its quality shops, with stores such as Pettigrew and Stephens, Copeland and Lye, Daly's, Hendersons and Watt Bros. Glasgow was a cinema-mad city at one time and Sauchiehall Street played its part in this, with the Regal, La Scala and Gaumont cinemas - the "Sound of Music" ran at the Gaumont for two and a half years. The Locarno Ballroom was also located on Sauchiehall Street and many a Glasgow romance started on the dance floor there.

There is plenty of variety for Glasgow shoppers in this photograph from a section of the south side of Sauchiehall Street in the 1950s. For the fashion conscious you could buy corsets from the corsetiere or budget priced clothing from C&A, who had been trading in Glasgow since the late 1920s. If music was your thing, you will recognise the familiar firm of J D Cuthbertson & Co, who were prominent in Glasgow from the 1880s. Known for the quality of their pianos, J D Cuthbertson, were later to move round the corner to Cambridge Street, before being taken over by Littlewoods chain stores. After all this you could sit down and have a cuppa at the Central Cafe.

Pictured left is a view along Candleriggs from almost 60 years ago. This was historically the area of the old city of Glasgow where candlemakers plied their trade, at a safe distance from the crowded tenements clustered around the High Street. As the city expanded in the eighteenth century it became a thriving thoroughfare itself, lined with tenements and businesses typical of Glasgow at that time.

Looking down Candleriggs from its northern junction with Ingram Street, stands St David's, later known as Ramshorn Kirk. It had been without a congregation for a long while before being purchased by Strathclyde University in 1983. The church dates from 1826, built in Gothic Revival style by an English architect, Thomas Rickman, whose plans featured the large central tower which dominates the structure.

Candleriggs is perhaps best known as the site of the City Halls, a musical venue operated by Glasgow City Council, home to the BBC Scottish Symphony Orchestra and a regular Glasgow performance base for the Scottish Chamber Orchestra. The old Candleriggs Fruit Market building at the corner of Candleriggs and Bell Street housed a market for many years. Towards the southern end of Candleriggs was the Goldbergs department store, which closed in 1991.

What a lovely couple the elderly pair made as they left the barrows and vans on Ross Street, having bought whatever provisions they could afford on their pensions. Born when Queen Victoria was on the throne, they had lived through the deaths of four monarchs, seen six on the throne, with four being crowned and the abdication of another. Motor cars were introduced to the streets and aeroplanes into the skies. Radio, cinema, gramophones and television were all once newfangled ways to entertain them and wonderful household appliances came along to replace the kitchen range, flat iron, mangle, dolly tub and sweeping brush. What changes they had seen and mostly as man and wife. The institution of marriage that bonded them together was under threat in 1967, as they walked arm in arm in clothing that suited them and ignored the dedicated followers of Carnaby Street fashion. In the swinging 60s free love was the recommendation of those whose first thoughts were of personal pleasure and not responsibility. It seemed to be the case that if you did not experiment with sex, drugs and rock and roll you were out of touch, but how many of those who then went on to burn their bras and embrace flower power can claim to have achieved the happiness and contentment that this couple had for all the world to see?

WORK & INDUSTRY

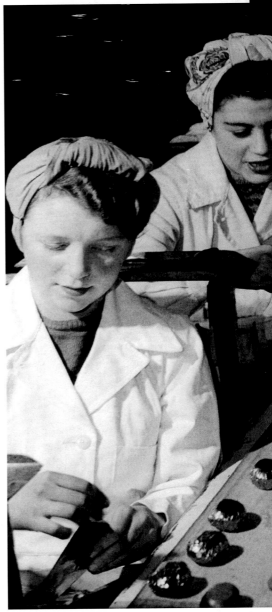

These Edison Accumulator vans, pictured above, belonging to the Electricity Department of Glasgow Corporation, were part of a small fleet in use just before the First World War. In 1901, Thomas Edison began developing a nickel-iron battery, based on an earlier Swedish invention. Its use in providing power for road vehicles was short lived. His batteries could be charged in half the time it took to re-energise lead-acid varieties and they were clean and initially effective. But, they performed poorly at low temperatures and were expensive to buy. Edison's most popular models were the GMC and the Detroit, the latter being particularly reliable when negotiating inclines.

Did you know?

Partick has been in existence since at least 1136 at various times being known as Perdeyc, Perthic, Perthec and Partic. Until the mid-1880s Partick had a drummer who would beat his drum every day at 5am, to get everyone up for work, and at 9pm to signify that it was time to go back to bed.

Easter will soon be here in the main photograph from 1951, and of course, all the kiddies will want their Easter eggs. So the Glasgow firm of Macmillan and Monro are seeing they get them by turning out three thousand, 2-ounce eggs an hour, on their up-to-date machines. Tens of thousands will find their way from this factory to all parts of the British Isles. This is one end of one of the conveyor belts with girls busy wrapping them in coloured foil.

In the photograph above, we can see the tranquil scene of workers leaving the Royal Ordnance Factory (ROF) at Bishopton in the 1940s. This picture belies the important and dangerous work that was carried out in these factories during wartime. There are few local people who did not know something of the work that was carried out on site, but little was said. The explosive and munitions work that went on there, was, 'in defence of the realm'. Bishopton was fully functional by April 1941 and, unbelievably, around 20,000 workers were employed there at its peak. It was one of sixteen similar explosives ordnance factories built by the Ministry of Supply during the Second World War.

Women working in the munitions factories were nicknamed 'munitionettes'. They worked long hours with shifts of 10-12 hours a day risking their health, and sometimes even their lives to make munitions, for less than £2 per week. Their commitment had a lasting impact on the war effort and sometimes changed their lives forever. The ROF site, which was privatised in 1984, finally ceased explosives production in 2002

foray into Cowlairs Co-op, or which other branch they patronised. The women packing the rations knew that the country was going through a truly bad patch as news from the battlefronts filtered through. Although the censors prevented the full story from reaching the general public, it knew that Singapore fell to the Japanese in February, the Luftwaffe had begun targeting Britain's historic towns in its 'Baedeker' raids and Rommel's panzer divisions had driven back the Allies in North Africa in May.

The women pictured left leaving the Twomax factory at 183 Rutherglen Road had just knocked off for the day, their time at the sewing machines done for another twenty-four hours. In the 1960s the clothing industry provided the inspiration for a hugely entertaining television sitcom, 'The Rag Trade'. Starring Peter Jones as the harassed boss, it also featured a strong comic performance each week by Miriam Karlin, playing a feisty shop steward. Any problem that the workforce encountered was greeted by a blow on Miriam's whistle and, with the call 'Everybody out', the girls marched from the cutting room for yet another strike.

The image to the left was captured inside the Scottish Co-operative Wholesale Society (SCWS) who had its headquarters on Morrison Street and was part of the movement that began life in a little grocer's shop on Toad Lane, Rochdale, Lancashire, in 1844. Buying and selling goods for its members, the society paid a regular dividend in the form of stamps, known colloquially as the 'divvy'. Before long the movement had spread across Britain, but in 1942 these Co-op workers had more on their minds than savings stamps. They were packing tea rations at the factory in Shieldhall and playing their part in the war effort. With a good eye for hygiene, in their neatly starched mobcaps and overalls, they carefully measured out each allowance that would be permitted to housewives undertaking their shopping

Although a comedy, 'The Rag Trade' had echoes of real life for industrial action and an inability to control the unions helped cost the Labour government the general election in 1970. However, these women belonged to the time when few of them had televisions, as the photograph is dated 1956. ITV had only been on the air since September 1955 and the Tories were part way through their 13 years of power. Twomax was established in 1922 by the McClure family and produced fashion goods, especially knitwear, for major stores and the mail order trade. It was later to go into liquidation with a loss of 150 jobs, but a rescue package was put together and, under the guidance of Martin Frost and three other associates, it was revamped with an investment of nearly £2,000,000.

Wholesalers, market stallholders, retailers and individual shoppers brought the road to a standstill as the lorries and vans unloaded their produce on the corner of Bell Street and Albion Street for the fruit and vegetable market, near Candleriggs in 1955. Barrows and trolleys were used to take it inside, but there was little chance of clearing it all through the doors in a short time. Anyone wishing to pass along the road had better replan his route, for no one was going to make way until the job was finished. There was too much to do and a large amount of competition to contend with as the traders vied with each other over price and quality. The market was held in the City Halls, where a bazaar first traded in cheese, fruit and vegetables in 1817. In 1841 the halls were built above the bazaar and were used for concerts, dances and lectures, becoming one of Glasgow's most important entertainment and cultural venues. The market ceased to function in 1969, though its structure still occupies part of the site. Candleriggs became a built up street in 1724, ending the work of the candle factories that had operated on the riggs (fields) that were once here. The candle manufacturers had previously been moved to Candleriggs from other parts of the city as they presented a fire hazard.

Ross and Liddell

The Property People

Ross and Liddell began managing property in Glasgow in the Victorian age. Founded by 'house factor' Alexander Barron in 1854, today the firm is one of Scotland's leading property specialists. As well as property management and maintenance, the business provides a comprehensive range of residential and commercial services. The name Ross and Liddell goes back to 1898.

In 2008, the country faced a financial crisis. Ross and Liddell was not immune, but coming out of recession the business has continued to thrive.

Ross and Liddell's office network increased in 2009 with the company opening in Dundee's harbourside. The new office allowed Ross and Liddell to offer clients in Dundee the same comprehensive residential letting service available in Glasgow, Paisley and Edinburgh.

Expansion in Dundee was soon followed by the opening of a new residential lettings and estate agency in Anniesland, in Glasgow. Keen to improve the service, in 2013, Ross and Liddell moved this office to the heart of Glasgow's West End which has been well received by clients.

In the same year Ross and Liddell acquired the business of B & B Property Management which had been servicing properties in Dumbarton, Alexandria, Helensburgh, Rhu, Cardross and Balloch since 1894.

The Paisley office also moved into new premises, in 2014. The Glasgow Road location provides excellent accommodation over four levels.

Ross and Liddell plays an active role in the Property Managers Association Scotland and this has allowed them to play a vital part in the development of the Property Factors Act, which was implemented in 2012.

The scheme gives home owners peace of mind when choosing an accredited property manager. All property management firms were required to seek formal registration and to meet set criteria to continue to trade. The changes have been positively received and Ross and Liddell continues to improve and enhance the service it provides to clients.

A big charity supporter, in 2011 Ross and Liddell launched its own Community Bursary, which aims to provide financial support to groups in the local communities in which it works. It has had an overwhelming response and to-date has provided funding to more than 80 organisations across Scotland.

Over the years, employee numbers have steadily grown to 88 and training continues to be a top priority - continuing professional development enables all Property Managers to keep up-to-date with the latest legislation and changes within the industry – as well as providing a fully compliant services to clients.

Top, left to right: *Brian Fulton, Director at Ross and Liddell, Joanne Knox, Property Manager, and Cllr Mark MacMillan, leader of Renfrewshire Council at the opening of the new Paisley office.* **Left:** *Irene Devenny, Managing Director, with Property Managers based in Glasgow.* **Above:** *Clovenstone Boxing Club, who received funding from the Ross and Liddell Community Bursary in 2012.*

J&M Murdoch & Son
Working for a Better Environment

Paper, Cardboard, Glass), Soil Recycling, Metal Recycling, Site Clearance, Liquid Waste Removal, Green Waste Disposal, Hazardous Goods Disposal, Skip Hire and Haulage.

Over 250 individual truck movements can be conducted in a single day; work goes on twenty-four hours a day, without restrictions. While most of the work is local to Scotland, Murdoch's operate over the whole of the UK, with the ability to do European work too, if required.

The company offers a wide range of waste-disposal services, ranging from skip trucks for handling household waste, tippers for 'muckaway' and demolition jobs, a waste transfer station for recycling, and has its own landfill site. The business also operates a number of tankers for the removal and disposal of liquid waste. There's also a fleet of heavy-haulage tractors and trailers which carry out Murdoch's other specialty, the movement of plant and machinery for other companies.

Today Murdoch's – J&M Murdoch & Son Ltd – is the UK's leader in Waste Management, Skip Hire, Waste Disposal and all forms of Recycling. Initially the business was formed to haul agricultural feeds/materials, it then developed into general haulage (Grants being large customer for whisky distribution). That side of the business lapsed due to increased fuel costs, regulations and changes in the customer base - then Skip Hire was added. At the outset, due to low landfill prices recycling wasn't the 'in thing'. By contrast today this is a major part of the business which now recycles some 89% of all materials received via its own Landfill Site, Material Recycling Facility and Transfer Stations.

Now based at Crofthead Industrial Estate, Lochlibo Road, Neilston, J&M Murdoch has been providing transport services and waste management, disposal and recycling for over 40 years. The company's services now include: Recycling (Wood,

Top left: *The Murdoch family: founders John and Margaret Murdoch (seated and second left back row) with sons John jnr (left) and Drew (right), and daughter Helen (second from right).* ***Left:*** *John with one of his earliest vehicles at Thornliemuir Farm, Paisley.* ***Above:*** *An early company van.*

In March 2014 the company got its new DryRecyclate Plant commissioned. It has been a substantial investment for Murdoch's, handling cardboard along with paper, cans and plastic. The firm had already been doing runs for Cardboard Only - collecting on regular schedules or providing an ad hoc service. Confidential Shredding is another service which will soon be available.

What became J&M Murdoch & Son Ltd was started in 1965 by John and Margaret Murdoch to carry animal feeds. It was a natural progression from John's agricultural roots. The business started out with haulage carrying feeds/agricultural supplies locally. Though now retired, both John and Margaret are still involved in the business.

Animal feed/hay and straw were some of the main products carried. The first lorry bought for £100, was used for transporting those animal feeds and agricultural materials, and later vehicles added to haul containers for Northern Ireland Trailers.

John Murdoch Snr's first truck was a Thames Trader. It was followed by Bedford trucks (costing £450) then by a Commer. His first new vehicle was purchased in April 1970 – a Dodge 16 ton gross weight, registration number VHS815H; it cost £3,000, today a similar vehicle would be £60,000.

When the business started there were no licences and driver regulations as there are today. A, B & C Operator Licences were the only thing needed: they worked on the basis of 'A' – Unrestricted - which required attendance in court with the customer to confirm and validate requirements, and, most-common, 'B' Limited Mileage – travel only within a 25 miles radius. With a 'C' one could only haul a customer's own goods – John Snr had two Contract 'C' customers – one being Robert Howie Goldie Ltd, which is still in business today.

At the outset Tommy Dollin (Margaret's brother-in-law) came to help. He would retire only in 2014 after 42 years with the firm. Also involved in the early days were Helen Dollin and Jimmy Philp. John Murdoch Snr was the driver and mechanic, before becoming Managing Director. Margaret looked after the office, scheduling, accounts, and finance before becoming Finance Director and Company Secretary. Others also played an important part in the business. Joe Mitchell was the first driver employed for the J&M Murdoch business, and worked for the company some 20 years. Frank Cargill was a milk boy for John Murdoch Snr from the age of 11 and then became a driver for him at the age of 17; he is still employed to this day as Traffic Manager. Frank Daly originally employed as 'Artic' driver, but latterly on 8-wheel tippers, has a 38 years service record. And Bob Kerr, employed as an 'Artic' driver when at Glenfield Road, is now N/S Foreman/driver.

John Murdoch Jnr, the founders' elder son, joined the business in 1977, his sister Helen in 1980, and in 1986 younger brother Andrew began work for the family firm.

Top left: The first vehicle to be painted in the Murdoch red and white. Left: J&M Murdoch's former Glenfield Road premises. Above: The fleet at Glenfield Road.

Helen worked in the office and on the 'skip desk' before becoming Director & Manager of Office & Skip Operations.

John, originally a driver and mechanic would become Director in charge of Fleet, Maintenance & Haulage. Andrew, who held many positions including vehicle painter, machine operator and driver, would eventually become Waste Management & Recycling Director.

In the early 1970s the firm were based at Thornliemuir Farm, Paisley, and operated just seven vehicles. The company moved in 1973 to Glenfield Road, Paisley, switching more into general haulage, transporting whisky, timber, fertiliser and containers. The fleet grew to 30 vehicles. The firm became a limited company in 1975 at the height of the Middle East oil crisis.

Many other economic difficulties would face the company. Unemployment rose from 5.3% of the working population in August 1979 to 11.9% in 1984. In the face of recession the Murdoch fleet was reduced from 35 vehicles to 18 and the company responded by diversifying, buying its first 'King Step Frame Trailer' to increase loads available to customers and bring in additional work.

The US Savings and loans crisis of 1990-91 saw the fleet reduced again, from 25 vehicles to 12.

In 1992 the company had opened its fourth Landfill Site – a major gamble to the small family business at the time, considering the economy and not knowing at the time that in 1996 landfill tax charges would be instigated by the government.

The fleet was downsized to 18 vehicles in order to specialise in plant transport, waste disposal and recycling. By 2008, however, the fleet had again grown to over 40 vehicles, however, an even worse recession was about to arrive.

The financial crisis of 2008-09, the deepest UK recession since the war, saw the Murdoch fleet reduced from 43 vehicles to 35 - and a three day working week introduced for staff. Belts were tightened and overtime, unnecessary costs and improvements were put on hold. Yet the changes made by the company a decade earlier would now begin to pay real dividends.

The move had been made in 1997 to the firm's present base, a former thread mill in Neilston. Crofthead Mill is one of the oldest mill buildings left standing in Scotland and it has shaped Neilston as it is today through its history.

Established in 1792 at the height of the industrial revolution, it was one of seven large mills that had formed along the banks of the River Levern between Neilston and the Dovecothall. Today it is a listed building, and is the home of J&M Murdoch though there are proposals for it to one day become part of a residential and retail development.

The mill is one of the largest complexes to have even been built in the area, and was described as being a small town itself in the early 1800s when the industry was at its peak.

Top left: Loading up Murdoch's first Low Loader purchased new in 1970. *Above:* One of the company's mini skip vehicles. *Below:* A Murdoch Scania of the 1980s.

Once employing hundreds of people from across the area, it sits just a few hundred yards from the heart of the village.

Several Neilston streets owe their existence to the mill. Originally owned by the Orr family, it was decided that more housing was needed to provide homes for the ever-expanding workforce at the growing factory, which at the start of the 20th century employed twice as many people as it had previously.

Lintmill Terrace, and its neighbouring streets of millhouses were created in 1904. The 400 homes formed much of what was Holehouse - a completely separate area of the Neilston parish that was not considered part of the actual village. Further expansion in the inter-war years saw Neilston and Holehouse join, and the borders of the village as it exists today began to form. The mill would finally cease production in 1992 after two hundred years, resulting in major staff redundancies and the bulk of the production being moved to a factory in Newton Mearns.

Today J & M Murdoch & Son Limited is still run from Crofthead Mill, Neilston. It is now headed by the founders' children John Murdoch junior, Andrew Murdoch and their sister Helen. From originally having just two staff at the outset it now has over a hundred, many of whom are family members, not least Jim

Davidson (Uncle), Kirsty Murdoch (Andrew's wife) Lesley Murdoch (John Jnr's wife), Ian and Fiona Murdoch (John Jnr's son and daughter), and John Allan (Helen's son).

Murdoch's is a family business through and through, and operates an 'open door' policy with its customers and employees. The firm gives a personal service and enjoys repeat business from a loyal base of existing customers alongside new customers who like the fact that there are no barriers in speaking to anyone – either on the phone or in person. The company takes pride in being a problem solver not a problem maker.

Main customer markets are as varied as the range of services now provided encompassing haulage and waste. Clients now include trade/commercial businesses, blue chip, construction, house builders, demolition, landscapers and general builders.

Top and inset: *A recent (top) and 1900s view (inset) of Crofthead Mill, home of J&M Murdoch.* ***Below:*** *A J&M Murdoch liquid waste tanker.*

The firm has dealt with a number of powered access and tarmacadam/road surfacing/improvement companies for over 20 years as well as UK construction and house building companies. Clients also include the general public who hire skips for home improvements.

No longer limited to Scotland, the full range of services is now supplied throughout the UK: - Skip Hire, Recycling Bins/Carts, Tipper Hire, Aggregates, Plant Transport, Waste Recycling (including bulk movement), Industrial Services (hazardous wastes), Tankers – fuelling, drain cleaning, septic tanks etc, Storage. And from late 2013 the latest addition to the range of services – Road Sweepers.

The vehicle fleet today is mainly Volvo, and currently stands at 50 vehicles. The business now concentrates on the niche markets for which the company has the specialist skills, vehicles and people. As old buildings come down materials need

removing and recycling, and as new ones go up, sites need machines and tippers and skips to prepare the way. It also runs a number of tankers for the removal and disposal of liquid waste.

There is also a fleet of heavy-haulage tractors and trailers which carry out Murdoch's other specialty, the movement of plant and machinery for other companies.

Top: *At the docks with a consignment of mobile hydraulic scissor lifts.* **Left:** *Murdoch tippers on a road surfacing project.* **Above:** *A selection of J&M Murdoch recycling bins.*

Technological advances have played a major part in Murdoch's development through the years, making possible more efficient and productive working methods. In recent years the introduction of SATNAV capabilities has enable the fleet to be tracked and co-ordinated by direct messaging from a fully computerised Control Desk via TOMTOM Driver – which even includes the facility to assess driving standards such as harsh breaking etc. Vehicles are now also running EURO 6, the most advanced, cleanest burning engines in the market, which helps reduce both emissions and running costs. Driver comforts including sleeper cabs, whilst modern driving accessories help reduce driver fatigue and ensure safe driving at all times.

Doing the best job one can to gain repeat business, and meeting and exceeding customer expectations both internally and externally is an intrinsic part of the Murdoch philosophy. Murdoch's ethos is to operate within the constraints of the family and not get greedy to be big – which, as we all know, isn't always best. And stick to what you know, not what you don't know, and look after the people who have supported you.

As a result Murdoch's has managed a sustainable 7% growth year on year, even if at times charges and haulage rates were reduced from previous years just to gain a baseline of good local work.

For the future, the company looks forward to continued growth, increasing the proportion of recycling materials, and embracing new technologies as they arrive.

Top and above: A J&M Murdoch road sweeper (top) and jetting truck (above). *Below:* A familiar sight to the people of Glasgow and beyond, a J&M Murdoch artic.

Cardowan Creameries

The Traditional Blend Giving True Scottish Value

It was the early years of the 20th century and Walter Kyle, a young engineer, left the shores of his native Scotland to prospect for gold in South Africa. He pegged a likely claim, sampled some quartz and found he had struck gold. However, his dreams of creating a vast fortune from the elusive metal were not to last, as after only a few years the gold-bearing seam disappeared and Walter Kyle returned to Scotland. It was then that he joined forces with a friend and found himself involved in producing gold bars of a different kind!

The years of the Second World War were difficult ones for the margarine industry, which came under the jurisdiction of the Ministry of Food, as wartime rationing required them to sell traders less than they wanted to buy. Walter Kyle's nephew Andrew returned from military service flying Spitfires in the RAF to face the next challenge, which came when rationing ended in 1954.

*Above: The transport fleet in the 1930s. **Below:** Early vans and their drivers outside the company's premises.*

His friend William Haddow was in the business of repackaging margarine into bars suitable for household use. The two men combined their skills and together started up a margarine manufacturing business in an abandoned munitions factory in Parkhead, Glasgow, an ideal location for storage of the barrels and drums of oils involved in the process. The business took off and Cardowan Creameries Ltd was incorporated in December, 1930.

At last housewives across Britain could tear up their ration books and Cardowan were able to sell as much margarine as they wanted, but frustratingly they had no existing customer base on which to build . Gradually, however, the 'King Cole' company logo, a whimsical play on the name Kyle, became a familiar sight around the streets of Glasgow as the company's fleet of delivery vehicles increased.

The year 1956 brought its own setbacks when a huge fire ripped through the building. The Glasgow Fire Service battled with the blaze, but could not save the factory from serious damage. The skeleton of steel beams, an inheritance from when Beardmore manufactured munitions on the premises during the First World War, survived, though the fire was serious enough to close the Cardowan factory for a year.

The past 84 years have seen many changes in the margarine production process. In earlier days whale oil, delivered in wooden casks, was a key ingredient of margarine. Today, the old wooden casks have given way to tanker loads of vegetable oils, which are stored in tanks within the factory. Over the years the Kyle family has remained committed to investing in the industry's future, replacing their machinery as new processes and modern technology were developed.

Today, nothing is left to chance, with computers metering the correct quantities of oils into compounding tanks, where other ingredients such as emulsifiers, salt, flavourings and colour are added. More modern margarine manufacturing methods have been introduced over the years, but where it is considered beneficial to the product, Cardowan have retained the traditional processes. For example, the chilling drum and complector method of producing pastry margarine is universally accepted to make a margarine which is far more tolerant of today's puff pastry making techniques, yet Cardowan Creameries are the only company in the United Kingdom still utilising this time proven method of production.

Above and below: *The 1956 fire ripped through the building. Glasgow Fire Service battled with the blaze, but could not save the factory from serious damage.*

The oils and fats used in producing the different blends of margarine are imported from all over the world. Each oil is refined and deodorised to remove all impurities before being delivered by tanker to the factory in Glasgow. The purified oil undergoes rigorous laboratory testing before being transferred to bulk storage tanks, ready for use in the manufacture of a wide range of products.

The Kyle family, now in its third generation with Walter Kyle's great-nephew John at the helm as managing director, have kept Cardowan Creameries as an independent family business, and are justifiably proud of their determination to stay at the forefront of innovation and new developments within the industry.

Above: *Production methods in the late 1980s.* *Right:* *The Cardowan Creameries premises in the 1990s.*

According to John Kyle, this kind of service is a key factor in the family firm's success, and Cardowan's individual blend of quality, service, price and reinvestment will allow it to continue to supply customers with the products that they require in an ever more demanding marketplace. After more than 80 years the desire to excel remains undiminished and they will continue to supply high quality, premium products with their unique combination of innovation and tradition for many years to come.

Left: A tanker delivering palm oil, 2014. Below: Modern factory machinery.

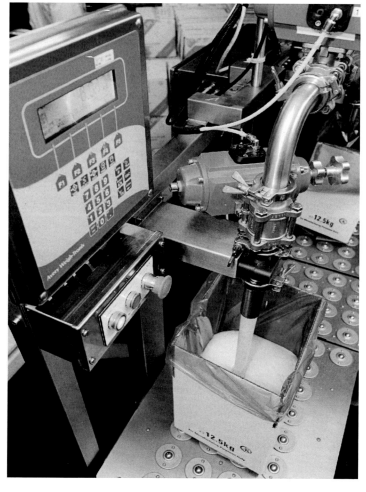

Indeed, in 2010 Cardowan Creameries were the first company in Britain to offer a range of bakery fats made using fully certified sustainable palm oil to food manufacturers, when it added fully segregated sustainable and mass balance cake margarines, pastry margarines and shortenings to its already extensive portfolio. It is of the utmost important to the Company that it procures raw materials that have been produced to the highest ethical and environmental standards.

The margarines and shortenings which are manufactured are continually evaluated in-house in the company's test bakery, where cakes and pastries of all kinds are produced to allow the skilled staff to evaluate the versatility and quality of their products.

Cardowan Creameries are suppliers to the baking, catering and food processing industries across the board, from the small independent baker to major food manufacturers. The wide range of different products reflects their differing requirements and demands.

Packed in 12.5 kilo boxes or pallet containers, products are despatched to destinations across Britain, Ireland and Europe. Customer care is a top priority, and in addition to the standard range of bakery fats, Cardowan are also able to offer customers bespoke products to meet particular characteristics or labelling requirements. Technical staff are available to provide advice, help with any problems, create solutions and assist customers with new product development.

THE DENHOLM GROUP
Proud of the Past, Ambitious for the Future

Many a stirring story has started with an office clerk running away to sea. The hardships which fate usually metes out, however, were avoided by young James Denholm, founder of J&J Denholm Ltd. As premature head of his family he started work in a law office aged fourteen. He loathed it but wisely learned, and saved, all he could. By the time he was twenty, in 1866, the determined youngster was established as a Factor and Land Agent in Greenock.

James was determined to build up a seagoing clientele among the Brixham schooners trading between London and Glasgow. By 1869, when his sixteen-year-old brother, John, joined him, James was registered as a Shipping Agent and Shipbroker. With phenomenal drive the brothers soon began outstripping their rivals.

The Denholms' first vessel was the David Sinclair, a 122 ton Brixham topsail schooner. The bank considered the brothers far too young to be taken seriously, but two local men knew the Denholms better and put up the £2,500. The David Sinclair ran coal to the West Indies and Americas and returned with grain, pine resin and sugar.

Sadly, in 1875, James Denholm died of tuberculosis. Six years later John Denholm married his first wife, Jane, and by 1882 the company had grown to twelve wooden sailing ships engaged in the West Indies trade. The change-over from sail to steam, by way of imperfect hybrid ships combining sail with steam engines whose coal took up profit-making cargo space, was by trial and error. But by 1882, when Denholm's purchased its first steel steamship the Carronpark, for £8,300, these problems had been resolved and the beautiful wooden sailing ships began to fade into history. As the modern fleet grew the old sailing vessels were sold off.

For the next century, and more, of Denholm's existence all its new ships bore the suffix '...park' at the end of their names. For example seven Denholm ships have proudly borne the name Mountpark. With true Scots thrift the ships' names were kept to two syllables as it was found that longer names cost more in telegraph communication charges!

Following the death of his first wife, John Denholm remarried, in 1891, another Jane, with whom he would have seven children, including the next pair of brothers, John and William, who would help build the Denholm empire.

Top left and left: Top left is the David Sinclair, the first ship owned by Denholms and pictured left is the log book for a journey made by the David Sinclair in 1874 from Brixham to Italy and on to New York. During the journey the ship was subject to storm damage and the Master, Mr Brittain, was later charged with the manslaughter of the ship's cook. *Below:* John and James Denholm c1870.

Royal Navy, whilst a third went to sea as an apprentice.

The immediate post-war years saw ships returned to the company flag, compensation paid for those lost, and the newer vessels equipped with wireless operated by a new breed of officer known as 'Sparks'. A new Denholm Shipping Company bought and sold ships, one of which had seen war service as a Q-ship, as the disguised armed-merchantmen submarine-hunters were known.

From 1921, sea-going trade witnessed a decade of depressions and fluctuations brought about by higher costs, strikes and falling freight rates. John Denholm, who now became President of the UK Chamber of Shipping, steered his company through these difficult years until, in 1934, by now an octogenarian, he handed the helm to his son, John. Increasing trade in the later Thirties saw the Denholm fleet established with nine vessels and another two on order when the Second World War broke out.

Once again, ships were requisitioned and staff called up. All but two company vessels were sunk, the majority by torpedo attacks from submarines, and both the Greenock and London offices were bombed in air

Jane died in 1901, after which John Senior, soon to be President of the Greenock Chamber of Commerce and Provost of Greenock, married her sister Jessie.

In 1909, the management of all Denholm ships was rationalised by bringing them under the unifying flag of The Denholm Line Steamers Ltd with a share capital of £42,800 in the days when the pound sterling was worth £100 today.

By 1913, John Denholm, aged 59, commanded a fleet of seven ships valued at £89,000. In 1914, the first year of the Great War, four of his vessels were requisitioned by the Government, while the Garvelpark, moored in Danzig, was seized by the Germans. Undeterred, Denholm's ordered three new ships equipped with electric light, a shipboard innovation at the time, at a total cost of £100,000. Meanwhile, two of John's younger sons saw service in the

raids. John Denholm was awarded the CBE for his service with the Ministry of War Transport, whilst his brother William commanded 77th Highland Field Regiment at Dunkirk and beyond.

Top left: The launch of the SS Garvelpark in 1901. The small boy on the front row is John C Denholm, who later became chairman of the company. Left: Lieutenant J C Denholm RNVR, on board HMS Ladybird in 1917.

The decision to rebuild the Denholm fleet after the war was regarded by many ship-owners as folly. As things turned out the Denholm brothers were able to make a success of the venture by wise, even lucky, buying and cost effective chartering, to rebuild their line to seven ships. They expanded into oil and ore carrying which later became dominated by the giant bulk carriers.

Post-war many independent family businesses were merging to provide economies of scale. First Denholm's allied itself with other Scottish companies, and then with Norwegian firms - eventually managing fourteen American-owned ships. Adapting to circumstances, the Denholms went in for ship management rather than ship owning and rapidly became one of the largest ship management concerns in the world. By the mid-1960s that fleet numbered 48 ships with a combined tonnage of 1,332,000 cwt.

Modern training, manning and management techniques to supply well-qualified and adaptable officers and crews enabled Denholm's to bridge the old ship-shore divide between seamen and managers. A new construction team supervised ship-building projects. In the 1970s, mini-bulkers of 3,000 tons were developed for short voyages and small loads, whilst another Denholm enterprise organised the Atlantic Bulkers Pool of 30,000 ton bulk-carriers operating as the 'tramp steamers' of yore to go wherever trade was. In the same decade, Denholm's managed the first British ships to be powered by jet aircraft type gas turbine engines which turned the biggest variable pitch propellers then fitted to merchantmen.

During the Seventies, Denholm's was managing about one per cent of the world's shipping tonnage. But trading conditions were changing, with others keen to emulate Denholm's success and to make use of international seamen and drive down costs. Against that backdrop, Denholm's sought to diversify.

The first diversification was seafood. Today, the seafoods activity is in two parts. The first consists of an investment in some 25 vessels around Scotland and Northern Ireland and a chandlery business to support them; the second part is a pelagic processing and freezing plant in Peterhead supplying mackerel and herring products worldwide.

Top: Mountpark, which was built in 1912, ran aground in the River Forth. Closer inspection reveals a crew member being brought ashore by breeches buoy. Left: The Vancouver Forest, built in 1969, under heavy ice.

Finally, Denholm's still operates an active ship brokerage business, covering dry bulk and specialist activity such as cable-laying. The management interests have been merged to form one of the largest global Ship Management operations, and whilst the only ship was sold in 2013, a new vessel is being ordered. So the Denholm Fleet moves on.

And as for the Denholm family. The business is still a family-owned and run group of companies. The fourth generation is currently at the helm, with another two sets of Denholm brothers in the business. Members of the fifth generation are also becoming involved.

There was also a return to Denholm's roots in ship agency. From the early Eighties, Denholm Shipping Services was built up; together with a number of acquisitions this now forms an international logistics business covering ships agency, warehousing, freight forwarding, stevedoring, transport and short sea shipping.

Denholm's also invested in support services for shipping and for the offshore industry. The painting of ships and offshore oil installations required additional skills in both cleaning and access (scaffolding), which quickly built into a multi-discipline industrial services company. This has in turn focused on contracting in the UK market (Denholm Industrial Services) and support to the oil and gas industry. The industrial services operation was responsible for the largest scaffolding site in Europe during the repairs to the Bidston Moss flyover near Liverpool, where Denholm's also provided cleaning, surface preparation and painting.

Meanwhile, Denholm Oilfield Services has expanded. It now comprises specialist cleaning, valve services, specialist oilfield logistics, heavy fabrication, light engineering and construction, electrical engineering, plant hire, maintenance services and recruitment. It operates in the UK, USA, Kazakhstan, the United Arab Emirates and Azerbaijan.

Today, the Denholm Group has an annual turnover in excess of £300m, shareholder-funds of over £100m, and employs more than 3,000 staff worldwide. After a century and a half the Group is rightly 'Proud of our past and ambitious for the future' – whatever it may hold.

Top left: Being loaded on to a barge is one of 44 different size superstructure platforms fabricated by Denholm Contracting Division for the Ruwais 3Road NGL Train project in the United Arab Emirates. Left Denholm Seafoods fishing boats 'Rose Bloom' and 'Boy John'. Below: On site with Denholm Oilfield Services Division.

Southern Coaches
Over 60 Years of Superb Coach Hire Across Scotland

On 20 November, 1950, a new business venture was launched in Newton Mearns: a general coach hire company was established under the now-familiar name of Southern Coaches. Two of the three founder directors were local men - William McIntyre and William Jamieson both lived in Newton Mearns, where, prior to founding Southern Coaches, the former had been a motor contractor and the latter a chemist. Robert Wallace, the third founder director, was a farmer from Stewarton, in Ayrshire.

The company commenced operations with just one vehicle, which was by no means new, but business clearly got off to a good start, because at a meeting of the directors, chaired by Mr McIntyre and held in the Registered Office at 139 St Vincent Street, Glasgow, on 16 March, 1951, some four months after the venture began, it was unanimously decided that a second bus should be acquired. This was to be a much newer Leyland Tiger, to be purchased at a cost of £3,640. Minutes of the meeting record that the transaction was to be financed by a bank loan from the Union Bank of Scotland in the amount of £2,750, and the remaining sum was to be covered by loans from two of the

directors, Mr Wallace and Mr Jamieson, who each agreed to lend £500 to the company, repayable at a rate of interest of six per cent a year. It is not recorded how long the Company was expected to take to repay its Directors; however, their confidence was fully justified and history has proved that the investment was a wise one.

Within a couple of years, the fleet had expanded a hundredfold and more; records for 1953 indicate that two Bedford coaches were acquired during that year, and Maudslay, Tilling Stevens and AEC Regal vehicles are also listed. As operations

expanded, larger premises were called for, and the company relocated from Newton Mearns to Lochlibo Road, Barrhead, from where it still operates. Meanwhile, the fleet continued to grow, with more Bedfords, an Albion Victor and a Commer Avenger being purchased before the end of the decade.

Top left: *Mr Robert Wallace, one of the original founders.*
Above: *The company's first vehicle - a Leyland Tiger.*
Below: *A Bedford Coach once owned by Southern.*

The company's reliable and affordable service proved popular with the local community, and it soon became a well-established concern. In the mid-1960s two of the founder directors, William McIntyre and William Jamieson, decided to resign from the company and go back to their original professions, leaving Robert Wallace to run the now-flourishing company. Robert was joined by his wife, Mary, who became company secretary.

As a family-run concern, the company continued to invest in its fleet, running a number of Ford and Bedford vehicles with Plaxton and Duple bodies, one Ford with a Burlingham body, and a Commer Avenger Mk III. Southern Coaches were a familiar sight on Glasgow's roads, and it was around this time that the company began to assign fleet names to individual coaches, painted on the rear as part of the livery; people may remember travelling on the Southern Pride, the Southern Queen, the Southern Monarch or the Southern Knight.

Southern Coaches' fleet carried on growing until at one point some 30 vehicles were in operation. Fewer vehicles are owned by the company today. The directors are constantly alert to the changing requirements of their customers, and current policy is to operate a smaller fleet, but to concentrate on investing in newer vehicles. In line with this policy, the present fleet consists of two mini-coaches and 12 large coaches with seating up to 57-passengers. To commemorate the company's 60th anniversary in 2010 a special registration number was ordered for a newly delivered coach. A diamond wreath was also added to the livery and can be seen adorning the coaches.

Day tours were very popular for the company and Mary was often found in a minibus in Pollok taking bookings, with long queues of eager travellers waiting to book their seats. On one occasion, 32 full coaches were bound for Saltcoats on the same day. However, with a decreasing interest in coach day tours, they no longer remained viable and the company stopped running them in 2012. Passengers and passers-by continue to stop and speak to drivers, recalling their fond memories of the day tours they went on as children.

The company continues its policy of concentrating on local work as much as possible, running a holiday service to Blackpool for September Weekend and operating a variety of luxury tours which cater for all tastes - from ski trips to golf tours, from school trips to senior citizens outings, and from distillery visits to business meetings and conference transportation. Other services include airport transfers, cruise liner shore excursions and city tours, and coaches are always available for private hire.

Sons Robert (Junior) and David Wallace joined their parents as directors of the company, and after the death of Robert (Senior) in 1992 Southern Coaches was run by the three remaining directors until the death of Mary in June 2011. The company continues to be owned by Robert (Junior) and David. It is very much a family business, experienced in meeting the needs and expectations both of the local community and of visitors to the region, and family and staff are proud that so many people, not only Glaswegians but tourists from further afield, have happy memories of holidays and excursions courtesy of Southern Coaches. The company is looking forward to the future in which it will continue to provide the friendly and reliable service upon which its reputation has been built.

Est. 1950

Top left: Southern's luxury coaches outside the 'Armidillo' in Glasgow. Centre: Southern Coaches' diamond wreath emblem. Below: A familiar sight to the people of Glasgow and beyond, one of Southern's Van Hool coaches.

Whyte & Mackay

Special in Every Way

Founded on the docks of Glasgow in 1844, Whyte & Mackay's iconic brand of Scotch whisky has remained true to itself and its founders James Whyte and Charles Mackay's pioneering spirit for over 170 years.

Today, when the traditional values of pride, integrity and style are often forfeited in favour of profit, expediency and celebrity, Whyte & Mackay Blended Scotch Whisky continues to be loved by Scots, who appreciate its rich, smooth flavour.

In 1844 most of Scotland was drinking cognac, and it was considered a bold move to invest in whisky, but Mr Whyte and Mr Mackay had the confidence to follow their beliefs. Using over 35 specially selected malts, they blended them together to form a distinctive 'Special' whisky.

Working on the philosophy of 'all good things come to those who wait', Whyte & Mackay uses a triple maturation process in the blending of their whisky.

Since the very beginning, the iconic symbol of Whyte & Mackay has been the double red lions. During the reign of David II, the Macgregors became an outlawed clan. Many of them assumed the name Whyte. As a mark of respect to the Macgregor/Whyte Clan, the founders of Whyte & Mackay took the lion from the Macgregor crest as their emblem. They then added the Lion Rampant of Scotland.

Whyte & Mackay's 'Double Lion' blend has its origins in the Glasgow firm of Allan & Poynter, founded in 1843 by John Poynter, a successful chemical manufacturer, and William Allan, a ham curer.

*Top left: Founders, Mr Whyte and Mr Mackay. **Above:** One of the first of Whyte & Mackay Special Selected Highland Whiskies. **Below:** An early staff photograph.*

The firm originally warehoused dry goods for the grocery trade. When the business changed hands the new owner, William Scott recruited two young men to help him, James Whyte and Charles Mackay.

By the end of the 1870s the firm was warehousing more and more whisky as wine and spirit merchants sought a substitute for brandy made unavailable by the grapevine disease, phylloxera. When William Scott died his widow sold the business to James Whyte and Charles Mackay. One of the conditions of the sale was that they were not to use the name Allan & Poynter, and thus the firm was renamed Whyte & Mackay. The young partners had no doubt that if they were to make a success of the venture they had to invest in whisky blending plant as soon as possible. It took two years to find and equip suitable premises in Robertson Lane, Glasgow. They received their first consignment of grain and malt whiskies and began blending to customers' orders. They later began blending on their own account for the export trade.

Charles Mackay died in 1919 and James Whyte in 1921. For small concerns like Whyte & Mackay the going was rough in the 1920s. Trade began to pick up in the late 1920s but this proved short-lived.

It was not until the 1950s, under the direction of James Whyte's two sons, Hartley and Alex, that the recovery was sustained with the end of voluntary rationing on the home market. In 1960 the company acquired Dalmore distillery in the north-east of Scotland and was renamed Dalmore, Whyte & Mackay. By 1965 Whyte & Mackay was the fifth most popular brand in Scotland.

The company became part of Sir Hugh Fraser's SUITS group in 1971. In 2005, Vivien Immerman bought the company and Whyte & Mackay was relaunched with a new look: the famous double lions rampant once more took centre stage. The original Whyte & Mackay blend was

renamed 'SPECIAL', as it was at the very beginning. In addition, 13, 19 and 22 years old aged blends with an extra year of maturation were added to the range.

Most distillers settle for one maturation, only Whyte & Mackay is triple matured to ensure a beautifully balanced blend. Firstly, our matured single malt whiskies are carefully selected by our Master Blender. Secondly we blend our malts together and allow them to mature in perfect harmony. Thirdly, our blend is returned to the cask and left to mature for several months. Only then is it ready for bottling.

This unique process not only guarantees a smooth, mellow and distinctive character, but more importantly it guarantees consistency, ensuring that every drop of Whyte & Mackay tastes as good as the first.

Top right An early 20th century view inside the bottling department. **Above left:** Old Whyte & Mackay products. **Below:** A selection from Whyte & Mackay's current range - more details of which can be found on the company's website: www.whyteandmackay.com

ACKNOWLEDGMENTS

The publishers would like to sincerely thank the following individuals and organisations for their help and contribution to this publication.

Herald and Times Group

Mirrorpix

dusashenka's photostream - www.flickr.com/photos/oldcinemaphotos/